Available Now!!!

Also by Bobbie Hinman

Bobbie Hinman, with Millie Snyder is the co-author of the immensely popular Lean and Luscious series, which consists of *Lean and Luscious* and *More Lean and Luscious.*

Each of these books includes over 400 delicious, low-cholesterol, low-fat recipes, comb-bound to lay flat for maximum cooking convenience. As in *Oat Cuisine*, each recipe includes at-a-glance nutritional breakdowns.

Available in Bookstores Everywhere!!!

Or, if you cannot find the book in your bookstore or prefer to receive the book by mail, send or call your order directly to Prima Publishing & Communications (see last page of this book).

Recipes shown on cover are:

"Oat-estroni" Soup	page 45
Italian Cornish Hens	page 64
Herbed Oats and Wild Rice	page 125
Onion 'n Oat Beer Bread	page 149
Raspberry-Almond Oat Bars	page 201

Important

This book is not intended as a substitute for your physician's advice. Its purpose is to show you how to add fiber to your meals while following a balanced diet, low in fat and rich in fruits, vegetables, grains, and beans.

Quantity discounts are available from Prima Publishing & Communications, P.O. Box 1260BH, Rocklin, CA 95677; telephone: (916) 624-5718. On your letterhead, include information concerning the intended use of the books and the number of books you wish to purchase.

U.S. Bookstores and Libraries: Please submit all orders to St. Martin's Press, 175 Fifth Avenue, New York, NY 10010; telephone: (212) 674-5151.

OAT CUISINE

**Over 200 Delicious Recipes
to Help You Lower Your Cholesterol Level**

Bobbie Hinman

Illustrations by Vonnie Crist

Foreword by
Peter O. Kwiterovich, Jr., M.D.
Director, Lipid Research
Johns Hopkins University

Prima Publishing & Communications
P.O. Box 1260BH
Rocklin, CA 95677
(916) 624-5718

Typography by Howarth & Smith Ltd.
Production by Robin Lockwood, Bookman Productions
Editing by Betty Duncan-Todd
Interior design by Renee Deprey
Cover design by The Dunlavey Studio

Prima Publishing & Communications
Rocklin, CA

Library of Congress Cataloging-in-Publication Data
Hinman, Bobbie.
    Oat cuisine / Bobbie Hinman.
      p. cm.
    "Over 200 delicious recipes to help you lower your cholesterol level."
    ISBN 1-55958-003-8
    1. Low-cholesterol—Recipes. 2. Cookery (Oat bran). 3. Oat bran—Therapeutic use.   I. Title.
    RM237.75.H56   1989
    641.6'313—dc20   89-37239
                                                                        CIP

89   90   91   92   RRD   10   9   8   7   6   5   4   3   2   1

Printed in the United States of America

Dedication

This book is dedicated, with love, to my mother. Thanks, Mom, for tirelessly testing and retesting recipes, giving me new ideas, and inspiring me to cook in the first place. Without you, I couldn't have done it.

Special Thanks

To all of the friends, relatives, and my husband's co-workers for taste-testing recipes and offering suggestions for new ones. Also to Mike and Lori for doing parts of this book that I couldn't do myself. And to Traci, Susan, and Mike for their willingness to eat all the leftovers. And, most of all, to Harry, for the love that made it all possible.

Contents

About the Author viii

Foreword by Peter O. Kwiterovich, Jr., M.D. ix

Introduction xi

Forms of Oats and Cooking Directions 1

Breakfast Ideas 9

Soups 43

Entrées 55

Meatless Entrées 77

Vegetables and Side Dishes 94

Breads 126

Yeast Breads 152

Muffins 164

Cakes and Pies 188

Puddings and Crisps 225

Cookies 243

Potpourri 263

Index 285

About the Author

Bobbie Hinman has been a pioneer in the field of low-fat cooking. When she first discovered, over 20 years ago, that her family had a hereditary cholesterol problem, she was a "typical high-fat gourmet cook." Determined to raise her family on a healthy low-fat diet, and aware of the fact that there were few, if any, teaching cookbooks available at the time, Bobbie set out to find ways to make healthy meals that were also tasty meals. She discovered a basic fact that she keeps referring to over and over. "The flavor is *not* in the fat!" By substituting low-fat ingredients for their higher-fat counterparts and using delicious combinations of spices and extracts, Bobbie has mastered the art of delicious, healthy cooking. Always learning and updating, she now turns her attention toward fiber as a way to further improve her family's health.

Bobbie is the co-author of the best-selling cookbooks, *Lean and Luscious* and *More Lean and Luscious*. She is constantly in demand as a speaker and cooking teacher and has been featured on several cable TV series.

In this book, as in her others, Bobbie shares her wealth of information with you.

Enjoy!

Foreword

Oat bran. Americans have been buying products made with oats so quickly that it is often difficult for stores to keep their shelves fully stocked. The avid interest of the American consumer in oats, and in particular, in the husk of oats, called oat bran, has been prompted by reports in the medical literature and in several recent popular books that oat bran can lower your blood cholesterol level.

If you are one of the many who are interested in using oat bran to lower blood cholesterol, you will find many creative, delicious recipes in *Oat Cuisine*. From soups to desserts, from vegetables and side dishes to breads and muffins, from entrées to shakes, this book has a full house of recipes.

If you have grown tired of the "an oat bran muffin a day" routine and are looking for ways to continue to supplement your diet with oat bran, this book is for you.

But there are other aspects of this cookbook that I found particularly appealing. For example, you will find at the end of each recipe the number of calories, the amount of protein, fat, carbohydrate, sodium, cholesterol and fiber contained in one serving. This nutritional information reflects the expertise of the author, Bobbie Hinman. This nutrient information serves as a reminder that the use of oat bran in your diet is meant to supplement a sound, nutritious, well-balanced diet, modified in total fat, saturated fat and cholesterol.

The recommended use of vegetable oil, particularly canola oil, an oil that is the lowest in saturated fat and that also contains an ample amount of monounsaturated fat, is a valuable addition to these recipes. In a diet meant to lower your blood cholesterol, the single most important factor is that it be low in saturated fat. Thus, these recipes as presented can be used very nicely in an overall low-saturated fat, low-cholesterol diet designed to lower your blood cholesterol level.

Another distinct benefit from many of these recipes is that they are high in total fiber. Americans generally eat too little fiber. Fiber is the undigested part of plant food that adds bulk to the diet promoting regular bowel habits, easing constipation, and providing a feeling of fullness and satisfaction after eating.

These recipes not only promote the use of fiber but water-soluble fiber such as oat bran. This is important since water-soluble fiber decreases blood cholesterol level while water-insoluble fiber does *not*. In addition to oat bran, other excellent sources of water-soluble fiber such as beans are also used in some of the recipes.

Oat Cuisine will provide an excellent addition to your repertoire of menus designed to help lower your blood cholesterol level through diet. If this is your goal, you should review your plans with your physician, and if possible, also with a qualified nutritionist to help you obtain the maximum benefit, and to minimize any risk.

Peter O. Kwiterovich, Jr., M.D.
Director, Lipid Research
Johns Hopkins University

Introduction

The past months devoted to an oat cookbook have proved to be quite an adventure. In a country where oats have traditionally been thought of as food for horses, why would I devote an entire book to oats? Well, oats are only part of the story. This book is really devoted to helping you add fiber to your meals, reduce the fat content, and still enjoy delicious foods. The adventure has been to find new and interesting ways to use oats in all forms, to combine them with other healthy ingredients, and to take full advantage of the unique flavor and texture that each form has to offer.

In recent years there has been quite a lot of publicity surrounding oats. The reason for this is that, first, studies have shown that a high-fiber diet may be our first line of defense against heart disease, and second, that a particular type of fiber—water soluble fiber—may significantly lower blood cholesterol levels. This type of fiber is abundant in oats and is also found in fruits and vegetables, such as apples, figs, prunes and carrots, and in legumes such as kidney beans, split peas and chick peas.

The other type of fiber—insoluble fiber—is found in whole grains such as cornmeal and whole wheat flour (especially wheat bran), and in fruits and vegetables such as broccoli, cabbage, raspberries and strawberries. This type of fiber seems to improve intestinal function and many researchers feel that it may aid in preventing some types of cancer.

There seems to be a strong enough relationship between a high-fiber diet and good health, and it is generally recommended by health professionals that we consume both types of fiber daily, with 20 to 35 grams being a total daily recommendation. Of that, it is felt that anywhere from 10 to 20 grams should be from soluble fiber.

It is important to keep in mind that no one single food can promote good health and protect us against heart disease. An oat bran muffin, for example, can't undo the effects of a high-fat diet. In creating this book, I have not only combined oats with other high-fiber ingredients but also have kept a watchful eye on the amounts of saturated fat, cholesterol, and sodium in each recipe. The following are a few guidelines that I followed in my recipes and that you can follow when adapting your own recipes:

- When vegetable oil is called for in a recipe, I choose an oil that is high in monounsaturated fat, such as olive oil or canola oil, or one that is high in polyunsaturated fat, such as safflower, or corn oil. All of these oils are low in saturated fat.

- By using a liquid sweetener such as honey, molasses or pure maple syrup in many of the dishes, I found that I was able to decrease the amount of oil in a recipe and still maintain the moistness desired.

- In place of whole eggs, I have used only egg whites because all cholesterol found in an egg is found in the yolk. Two egg whites will work in place of one egg, or, if you prefer, a commercial egg substitute can be used.

- Whenever dairy products are called for, I use only the low-fat varieties such as skim milk, nonfat yogurt, low-fat cottage cheese and part-skim ricotta cheese.

- To limit the amount of sodium in each recipe I have used salt-free products where available and have only included salt in a recipe where I felt it was essential to the flavor of the dish. Usually my instructions are "salt and pepper to taste." My personal recommendation is that you taste first and add salt sparingly.

- To further increase the amount of fiber in my recipes I have recommended *unpeeled* fruits and vegetables wherever possible. (Be sure to scrub them well.) I have also used whole wheat flour, which contains more fiber than all-purpose flour, in most of the baked goods.

Nutritional Analysis

This book provides a nutritional analysis for each recipe. The recipes have been analyzed for calories, protein, fat, carbohydrates, sodium, cholesterol and dietary fiber. When there is a choice of two ingredients, such as "salt-free, or regular tomato sauce," the breakdown is based on the first one mentioned. It is important to note that all nutritional analysis is approximate and may vary slightly depending on the brands of food that are used. Ingredients listed as "optional" have not been included in the analyses. If a recipe contains a "trace" of a particular item (less than 1/2 gram of protein, fat, carbohydrate, or fiber, or less than 1/2 milligram of sodium or cholesterol) the number will be listed as zero. The number of grams of fiber listed reflects the total amount of dietary fiber in each serving.

It is my goal to have this information help you to plan a healthy, balanced diet.

Forms of Oats and Cooking Directions

O*ats are available in several* different forms. Of them, oat bran is the most concentrated source of soluble fiber. However, remember that other forms of oats still contain abundant amounts of this type of fiber and can offer the same possible cholesterol-lowering effects when used as part of a healthy, low-fat diet. Part of the adventure in writing this book was in discovering the definitive flavor and texture that each form has to offer. In this section, you will learn about the basic forms of oats and how to cook them. For your convenience, I have also included microwave instructions.

Some forms of oats are available in grocery stores. The others are found in health food stores. All forms of oats, like most other grains, will keep for a long time if stored in air-tight containers in the refrigerator.

So, join me in my adventure, and let me help you discover the true versatility of this wonderful grain.

Oat Bran

Oat bran is the outer covering of the oat and contains the highest concentration of soluble fiber. It is a part of all other oat forms and is also available by itself (often called oat bran cereal). It can be cooked with water, juice, or milk for a nutritious breakfast cereal or be used to replace part of the flour in many bread, muffin, cake, and cookie recipes. Oat bran can be found in the cereal section of most grocery stores.

Makes 4 servings (1 cup each serving)

Basic cooking directions:
4   cups water
1-1/3 cups oat bran

Bring water to a boil over medium heat. Briskly stir in oat bran, using a fork or wire whisk, and cook 1 to 2 minutes, stirring.

To microwave 1 serving:
Combine 1 cup of water and 1/3 cup of oat bran in a 2-cup microwavable bowl. Microwave, uncovered, on high (100% power) for 2 minutes. Stir and continue to cook on high for 1 minute more or until desired consistency. Stir before serving.

Serving suggestions for oat bran:
- Serve as a breakfast cereal, topped with cinnamon or fruit.
- Add to meatloaves or burgers.
- Use it to replace some of the flour in cakes, breads, and muffins.
- Add it to fruit shakes.
- Use as a thickener for sauces and pâtés.
- Use it to replace part of the graham cracker cumbs in pie crusts.

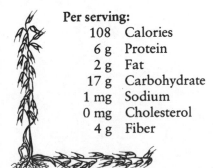

Per serving:
108	Calories
6 g	Protein
2 g	Fat
17 g	Carbohydrate
1 mg	Sodium
0 mg	Cholesterol
4 g	Fiber

Rolled Oats

*Rolled oats are flattened oats, or flakes, that many of us
have eaten since childhood. They cook quickly so there's
no need to buy the "quick" or "instant" varieties that are
sometimes processed or sweetened. Processing reduces the
nutritional value of the oats. (If you already have quick-
cooking oats, they can be used in most recipes in place of
rolled oats.) Besides breakfast cereal, rolled oats can be
used in cakes, cookies, breads, and a large variety of other
dishes. Look for rolled oats in the cereal section of most
grocery stores.*

Makes 4 servings (2/3 cup each serving)

Basic cooking directions:
3   cups water
1-1/3   cups rolled oats

Bring water to a boil over medium heat; stir in oats and cook 5
minutes, stirring occasionally. Cover, remove from heat, and let
stand 5 minutes.

To microwave 1 serving:
Combine 3/4 cup of water and 1/3 cup of oats in a 2-cup microwavable bowl. Microwave, uncovered, on medium (50% power) for
5 minutes or until cereal reaches desired consistency. Stir before
serving.

Serving suggestions for rolled oats:
- Serve for breakfast with your favorite topping.
- Add to meatloaves or burgers.
- Use them to replace part of the flour in cakes and breads.
- Sprinkle over fruit and bake for delicious "crisps."
- Add to soups in place of rice.
- Toast until brown; sprinkle on chicken or fish before baking.
- Make delicious cookies.
- Add texture and fiber to pancakes and waffles.

Per serving:

103	Calories
4 g	Protein
2 g	Fat
18 g	Carbohydrate
1 mg	sodium
0 mg	Cholesterol
3 g	Fiber

Whole Oats (Groats)

*Whole oats are natural, whole oats with only the outer
husks removed. They can be cooked in water, broth, or
juice and served as a delicious alternative to rice. Groats
can also be cooked with other grains such as rice, barley,
buckwheat, or wheat berries. Look for groats in health
food stores and in large grocery stores.*

Makes 6 servings (1/2 cup each serving)

3   cups water
1   cup whole oats

Combine water and oats in a large saucepan; bring to a boil over
medium heat. Reduce heat, cover, and cook 40 to 45 minutes, stirring occasionally. Drain.

To microwave:
Combine water and oats in a 2-quart microwavable bowl. Microwave, uncovered, on high (100% power) for 10 minutes. Then microwave on medium (60% power) for 25 minutes.

Serving suggestions for cooked groats:
• Serve as a side dish, topped with spaghetti sauce.
• Top with stir-fried vegetables.
• Add to meatloaves or burgers.
• Serve for breakfast, topped with raisins, cinnamon, or fruit.
• Use in place of rice in rice pudding.
• Add to your favorite soup or stew.
• Mix with beans and low-fat cheese for a hearty casserole.

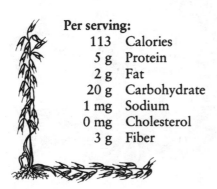

Per serving:
    113   Calories
    5 g   Protein
    2 g   Fat
    20 g Carbohydrate
    1 mg Sodium
    0 mg Cholesterol
    3 g   Fiber

Steel-Cut Oats

Steel-cut oats are whole oats that have been cut into several small pieces. They take less time to cook than whole oats, and, because they are only slightly processed, steel-cut oats contain most of their original vitamins. They make a thick, hearty breakfast cereal and a wonderful addition to soups and stews. Steel-cut oats can be found in health food stores.

Makes 6 servings (1/2 cup each serving)

Basic cooking directions:
3-1/2 cups water
1   cup steel-cut oats

Bring water to a boil in a medium saucepan. Add oats, reduce heat, and simmer 20 minutes, stirring occasionally. Remove from heat, cover, and let stand 5 minutes. Stir before serving.

To microwave 1 serving:
Combine 3/4 cup of water and 3 tablespoons of steel-cut oats in a 2-1/2-cup microwavable bowl. Microwave, uncovered, on medium (50% power) for 12 minutes or until desired consistency is reached.

Serving suggestions for steel-cut oats:
- Serve for breakfast, topped with cinnamon, raisins, or fruit.
- Add to soups or stews.
- Soak oats and add to bread dough for a crunchy texture.
- Cook and add to chili or burritos.
- Place cooked oats in blender with fruit for a thick, "instant" pudding.

Per serving:
113	Calories
5 g	Protein
2 g	Fat
20 g	Carbohydrate
1 mg	Sodium
0 mg	Cholesterol
3 g	Fiber

Oat Flour

Oat flour is made by grinding whole oats. It is a soft flour that gives baked goods a moist, velvety texture. By itself, oat flour will not rise because it contains no gluten. Therefore, it is usually mixed with wheat flour in cakes, breads, and muffins. Because oats contain a natural antioxidant, oat flour seems to keep baked goods fresher longer. Look for oat flour in most health food stores.

If you are unable to obtain oat flour, you can make your own by placing rolled oats in a blender and blending until the consistency of fine flour. Generally, 1-1/4 cups of rolled oats will yield 1 cup of oat flour.

Serving suggestions for oat flour:
- Use it to replace one-fourth to one-third of the flour in baked goods.
- Add it to casseroles as a thickener.
- Use it to thicken sauces and gravies.
- Replace part of the wheat flour in pancakes and waffles.

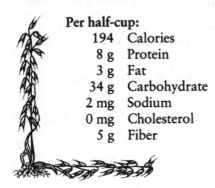

Per half-cup:

194	Calories
8 g	Protein
3 g	Fat
34 g	Carbohydrate
2 mg	Sodium
0 mg	Cholesterol
5 g	Fiber

Breakfast Ideas

When we think of oats and oat products, most of us think of breakfast. Traditionally, this is where oats have always been served. It's so easy to add the high fiber of oats to breakfast foods. Oats, in any form, can be cooked and topped with cinnamon, maple syrup, or your favorite fruit topping. Oats can also be cooked in combination with other grains for increased texture, flavor, and nutrition.

Many of the recipes in this section can be prepared at night and either slow-cooked or refrigerated overnight. What a treat to wake up in the morning to a convenient breakfast that's ready when you are.

For added fiber, try topping cooked oats, in any form, with any of the following nutritious toppings:

- Sliced bananas
- Fresh or frozen (unsweetened) berries such as blueberries, raspberries, or strawberries
- Chopped dried fruit such as prunes, dates, figs, apricots, peaches, or pears
- Raisins
- Sunflower seeds (unsalted, raw or dry-roasted)
- Shredded, unpeeled apples or pears
- "Streusel" topping of wheat germ and cinnamon

To make a nutritious breakfast and enjoy a wonderful "oaty" flavor and texture, try these suggestions:

- Combine oat bran, half and half, with Cream of Wheat® or cornmeal for a nutritious, hot, cooked cereal.
- Replace some of the flour in your favorite pancake recipe with oat flour or rolled oats.
- Cook oat bran or rolled oats in fruit juice instead of water.
- Soak rolled oats in skim milk or fruit juice in the refrigerator overnight and enjoy an unusual cold breakfast cereal.
- Cook steel-cut oats with cracked wheat (bulgur) or buckwheat groats for a hearty breakfast with lots of texture and flavor.
- For a rich creaminess, stir nonfat dry milk or nonfat yogurt into any form of cooked oats. Top with fruit for a delicious breakfast treat.

- Fill a crockpot with either rolled oats, steel-cut oats, or whole oats (groats). Add water, fruit, and cinnamon and cook overnight.

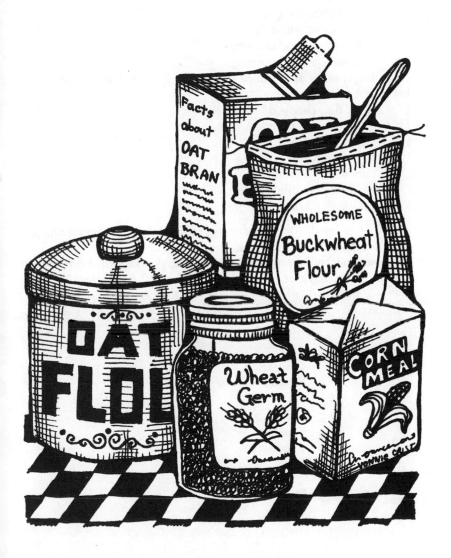

Muesli

This is our family's favorite version of the traditional Swiss breakfast cereal. Just mix and chill.

Makes 6 servings

1	cup rolled oats
3	tablespoons oat bran
3	tablespoons wheat germ
1/2	teaspoon ground cinnamon
1/8	teaspoon ground nutmeg
1	large, sweet apple, unpeeled, coarsely shredded (1 cup)
1/4	cup raisins
2	dried figs, chopped*
1/4	cup slivered almonds
1/3	cup apple juice
1	cup skim milk
1/3	cup water
2	teaspoons vanilla extract
1	tablespoon honey

In a large bowl, combine dry ingredients. Add remaining ingredients, mixing well.

Cover and chill overnight. Serve cold. (Cereal will keep several days in the refrigerator.)

*An easy way to chop dried fruit is to snip it with kitchen shears.

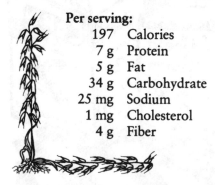

Per serving:

197	Calories
7 g	Protein
5 g	Fat
34 g	Carbohydrate
25 mg	Sodium
1 mg	Cholesterol
4 g	Fiber

Orange Oatmeal

*This is a real breakfast treat—oatmeal cooked with
orange juice instead of water. For a special touch, top
with a sprinkling of cinnamon and a little maple syrup.*

Makes 2 servings

1/2	cup water
1	cup orange juice (unsweetened)
2/3	cup rolled oats

Bring water and orange juice to a boil in a small saucepan over
medium heat. Stir in oats. Cook 5 minutes, stirring frequently.

Remove from heat, cover, and let stand 5 minutes.

Serve hot.

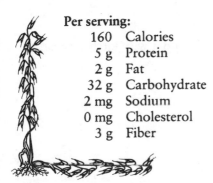

Per serving:

160	Calories
5 g	Protein
2 g	Fat
32 g	Carbohydrate
2 mg	Sodium
0 mg	Cholesterol
3 g	Fiber

Orange Fruit Treat

This delicious no-cook breakfast combines orange juice, oats, raisins, and dried apricots for an unusual taste treat. Serve it plain or top it with low-fat cottage cheese.

Makes 4 servings

1-1/4   cups rolled oats
1/4   cup raisins
1/4   chopped, dried apricots (or mixed dried fruit)*
1   cup orange juice (unsweetened)
1/3   cup water
1   teaspoon sugar

In a medium bowl, combine all ingredients. Mix well, cover, and chill overnight.

Serve cold.

*An easy way to chop dried fruit is to snip it with kitchen shears.

Per serving:
176   Calories
5 g   Protein
2 g   Fat
37 g   Carbohydrate
4 mg   Sodium
0 mg   Cholesterol
4 g   Fiber

Crockpot Oatmeal

*There's nothing like waking up to the aroma of oats,
apples, raisins, and cinnamon drifting through the house!*

Makes 6 servings

1-1/2 cups rolled oats
3-1/2 cups water
1   large apple, unpeeled, chopped (1 cup)
1/4   cup raisins
3   tablespoons firmly packed brown sugar
1-1/2 teaspoons ground cinnamon
1   teaspoon vanilla extract

In a large crockpot, combine all ingredients. Turn on low setting,
cover, and cook 6 to 8 hours or overnight.

Per serving:

143	Calories
4 g	Protein
1 g	Fat
30 g	Carbohydrate
4 mg	Sodium
0 mg	Cholesterol
3 g	Fiber

Granola

This delicious cereal also doubles as a handy snack. Try it sprinkled over applesauce or ice milk for a special treat or top it with raisins and fruit juice for a nutritious breakfast.

Makes 8 servings (1/3 cup each serving)

2	cups rolled oats
1/4	cup wheat germ
1/4	cup oat bran
1/4	cup firmly packed brown sugar
1-1/2	teaspoons ground cinnamon
1/2	cup orange juice (unsweetened)
2	tablespoons vegetable oil
1	teaspoon vanilla extract
1-1/2	teaspoons almond extract

Preheat oven to 300°.

Lightly oil a 10 × 15-inch baking pan or spray with a nonstick cooking spray.

In a large bowl, combine oats, wheat germ, oat bran, brown sugar, and cinnamon. Mix well.

In a small bowl, combine remaining ingredients. Add to oat mixture, mixing until all ingredients are moistened.

Spread mixture evenly in prepared pan.

Bake 30 to 35 minutes, until lightly browned, stirring every 10 minutes. (Be sure to watch carefully toward the end of the cooking time to prevent burning because oven temperatures vary.)

Remove from oven, break up any lumps that may have formed, and cool in pan on wire rack.

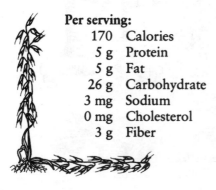

Per serving:

170	Calories
5 g	Protein
5 g	Fat
26 g	Carbohydrate
3 mg	Sodium
0 mg	Cholesterol
3 g	Fiber

Hot Granola Breakfast

Try this unusual cereal with the Granola on page 16. It has a toasty flavor, with the sweetener already built in. (Commercial granolas will also work, but read the labels carefully because many of them are loaded with fat.)

Makes 2 servings

1	cup water
1/2	cup apple juice
2/3	cup granola

Bring water and juice to a boil in a small saucepan over medium heat. Stir in granola. Cook 5 minutes, stirring frequently.

Remove from heat, cover, and let stand 5 minutes.

Serve hot.

Add raisins or chopped dried fruit for added flavor and fiber.

Per serving:
199	Calories
5 g	Protein
5 g	Fat
33 g	Carbohydrate
5 mg	Sodium
0 mg	Cholesterol
3 g	Fiber

Peaches 'n Creme Casserole

Elegant enough for a Sunday brunch, this creamy casserole is a different way to enjoy your breakfast oatmeal. It can be enjoyed as is or topped with skim milk or maple syrup.

Makes 6 servings

1-1/2	cups rolled oats
1-1/2	cups thinly sliced peaches, peeled (canned peaches, packed in juice, can be used)
1/4	cup sugar
2	egg whites
2	teaspoons vanilla extract
1/4	teaspoon almond extract
3	cups skim milk

Preheat oven to 350°.

Lightly oil an 8-inch square baking pan or spray with a nonstick cooking spray.

In a large bowl, combine oats, peaches, and sugar. In another bowl, combine remaining ingredients. Beat with a fork or wire whisk until blended. Add to oat mixture, mixing well.

Place mixture in prepared pan.

Bake, uncovered, 50 minutes.

Serve hot. (Leftovers are good cold or can be reheated in an oven or microwave.)

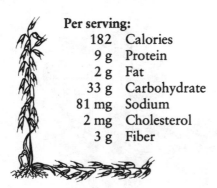

Per serving:

182	Calories
9 g	Protein
2 g	Fat
33 g	Carbohydrate
81 mg	Sodium
2 mg	Cholesterol
3 g	Fiber

Apple Oatmeal

*This is a quick, easy way to spark up your oatmeal. The
apple adds extra flavor and fiber.*

Makes 4 servings

2-1/2   cups water
2   large, sweet apples, unpeeled, coarsely shredded (2 cups)
1-1/3   cups rolled oats
1/4   teaspoon ground cinnamon
1/4   teaspoon ground nutmeg

In a medium saucepan, combine water and apples. Bring to a boil
over medium heat.

In a small bowl, combine oats and spices, mixing well. Stir into
boiling water. Reduce heat to medium-low and cook 5 minutes, stirring frequently.

Serve hot, sprinkled lightly with brown sugar or drizzled with
maple syrup.

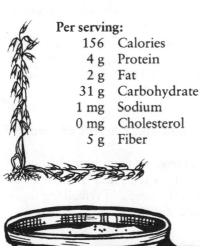

Per serving:
- 156 Calories
- 4 g Protein
- 2 g Fat
- 31 g Carbohydrate
- 1 mg Sodium
- 0 mg Cholesterol
- 5 g Fiber

Italian Oatmeal Patties

We love to serve these unique patties for brunch. They're a wonderful, cholesterol-free substitute for Spanish omelets.

Makes 6 servings

Patties:
3   cups water
1-1/2 cups rolled oats

Italian Sauce:
2   tablespoons olive oil
1   large onion, sliced
1   large green pepper, sliced
1   1-pound can salt-free (or regular) tomato sauce
1/2   teaspoon dried oregano
1/2   teaspoon dried basil
1/8   teaspoon garlic powder

Lightly oil an 8-inch square baking pan or spray with a nonstick cooking spray.

Bring water to a boil in a medium saucepan over medium heat. Add oats and cook 10 minutes, stirring frequently, until thick.

Spread mixture in prepared pan. Let cool and then cover and refrigerate overnight.

To prepare sauce:
(Sauce can either be prepared ahead and reheated or prepared just before serving):

Heat oil in a large nonstick skillet over medium heat. Add onion and pepper. Cook 5 to 10 minutes, until tender. Add water, if necessary, to prevent sticking. Reduce heat to low, add remaining ingredients, cover, and simmer 10 minutes.

To prepare patties:
Preheat a nonstick skillet or griddle over medium heat. Oil it lightly or spray with a nonstick cooking spray. Cut chilled oatmeal into 6 rectangular pieces. Place in preheated skillet. Cook until squares are crisp on both sides, turning them several times.

Spoon sauce over patties to serve.

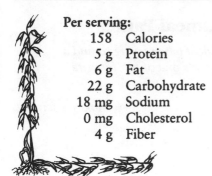

Per serving:

158	Calories
5 g	Protein
6 g	Fat
22 g	Carbohydrate
18 mg	Sodium
0 mg	Cholesterol
4 g	Fiber

Breakfast Oatmeal Patties

I discovered this dish by accident when trying to find a use for leftover oatmeal. Now it's one of our favorite breakfasts.

Makes 6 servings

3	cups water
1-1/2	cups rolled oats
1	teaspoon vanilla extract
	Ground cinnamon

Lightly oil an 8-inch square baking pan or spray with a nonstick cooking spray.

Bring water to a boil in a medium saucepan over medium heat. Add oats and cook 10 minutes, stirring frequently, until thick. Remove from heat and stir in vanilla extract.

Spread mixture in prepared pan. Let cool and then cover and refrigerate overnight.

To prepare patties:

Cut chilled oatmeal into 6 pieces. Preheat a nonstick skillet or griddle over medium heat. Oil it lightly or spray with a nonstick cooking spray. Place patties in skillet and cook until crisp on both sides, turning them several times.

Sprinkle with cinnamon and serve with maple syrup or your favorite jam.

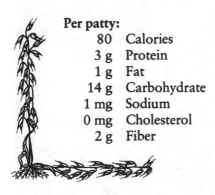

Per patty:

80	Calories
3 g	Protein
1 g	Fat
14 g	Carbohydrate
1 mg	Sodium
0 mg	Cholesterol
2 g	Fiber

Orange Oat Bran

In place of orange juice, try any of your favorite juices. A favorite in our family is orange–pineapple juice. We top it with a sliced banana and it tastes very tropical.

Makes 2 servings

1   cup water
1   cup orange juice
2/3 cup oat bran

Bring water and orange juice to a boil in a small saucepan over medium heat. Add oat bran, stirring briskly with a fork or wire whisk to keep cereal from forming lumps. Cook 1 to 2 minutes, stirring frequently.

Serve hot.

Sprinkle lightly with cinnamon or brown sugar, if desired.

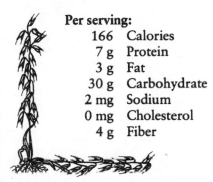

Per serving:
166	Calories
7 g	Protein
3 g	Fat
30 g	Carbohydrate
2 mg	Sodium
0 mg	Cholesterol
4 g	Fiber

Applesauce and Oat Bran

Mix this cereal at night for a refreshing, cold way to enjoy oat bran in the morning.

Makes 2 servings

2/3   cup oat bran
2/3   cup applesauce (unsweetened)
1   cup skim milk
1/4   teaspoon ground cinnamon
       Dash nutmeg

Combine all ingredients in a small bowl. Mix well, cover, and refrigerate overnight.

To serve, stir and sweeten to taste with brown sugar or maple syrup. Add raisins or other fresh or dried fruit, if desired. (This cereal can also be heated, if you prefer.)

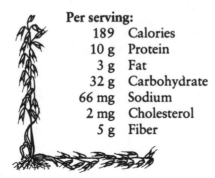

Per serving:
189   Calories
10 g   Protein
3 g   Fat
32 g   Carbohydrate
66 mg Sodium
2 mg   Cholesterol
5 g   Fiber

Raisin Bran Cereal

This steamy hot cereal combines two kinds of bran for a high-fiber breakfast that tastes like a bran muffin in a bowl.

Makes 4 servings

4	cups water
1	cup oat bran
1/3	cup wheat bran
1/2	teaspoon ground cinnamon
1/3	cup raisins

In a medium saucepan, bring water to a boil over medium heat.

Combine remaining ingredients and mix well. Add to boiling water, stirring briskly with a fork or wire whisk to keep cereal from forming lumps.

Reduce heat to low and simmer 5 minutes, stirring constantly.

Serve hot, sprinkled with brown sugar or maple syrup.

Per serving:

133	Calories
5 g	Protein
2 g	Fat
24 g	Carbohydrate
2 mg	Sodium
0 mg	Cholesterol
5 g	Fiber

Yogurt and Oat Bran Breakfast

*Mix this tasty cereal before you go to bed and simply add
your favorite fruit in the morning. It's a new way to enjoy
oat bran for breakfast.*

Makes 2 servings

1/3	cup oat bran
1	cup plain nonfat yogurt
1/3	cup skim milk
1/4	teaspoon lemon extract
1/4	teaspoon vanilla extract
1	tablespoon sugar

Fruit suggestions: raisins, sliced strawberries, blueberries,
sliced peaches, crushed pineapple, sliced banana

In a small bowl, combine all ingredients. Mix well. Cover and
chill overnight.

Serve cold, topped with your favorite fruit.

Per serving:

161	Calories
11 g	Protein
1 g	Fat
25 g	Carbohydrate
108 mg	Sodium
3 mg	Cholesterol
2 g	Fiber

Cornmeal Breakfast Combo

A unique combination of cornmeal and oat bran, this nutritious breakfast is packed with vitamins and fiber. We like it topped with a little maple syrup or molasses.

Makes 2 servings

1/3	cup oat bran
1/3	cup yellow cornmeal
1/2	teaspoon ground cinnamon
1/4	cup raisins (or any chopped dried fruit)
2	cups water

In a small bowl, combine oat bran, cornmeal, cinnamon, and raisins. Mix well.

Bring water to a boil over medium heat. Slowly add oat bran mixture, stirring briskly with a fork or wire whisk to prevent lumps.

Reduce heat to low and simmer, uncovered, 5 minutes, stirring frequently.

Per serving:

193	Calories
5 g	Protein
2 g	Fat
41 g	Carbohydrate
3 mg	Sodium
0 mg	Cholesterol
4 g	Fiber

Almond–Oat Bran Breakfast Treat

*Spread the top of this molded loaf with raspberry jam,
sprinkle a few slivered almonds, and you'll see why we
call it a breakfast "treat."*

Makes 4 servings

1-1/2	cups water
1/2	cup oat bran
1	tablespoon cornstarch
1/4	cup water
2	tablespoons honey
1-1/2	teaspoons vanilla extract
1/4	teaspoon almond extract
1/4	teaspoon ground cinnamon
1/4	cup raisins
1/4	cup slivered almonds
	Raspberry jam (optional)

Line a 4 × 8-inch loaf pan with plastic wrap, letting the edges
hang over the sides of the pan.

Bring the 1-1/2 cups of water to a boil over medium heat. Add
oat bran, stirring briskly with a fork or wire whisk. Cook 3 minutes,
or until thick, stirring frequently. Remove from heat.

In another small saucepan, combine cornstarch and 1/4-cup water, stirring until cornstarch is dissolved. Add honey, extracts, and
cinnamon. Cook over medium heat, stirring, until mixture comes to
a boil. Boil, stirring, 1 minute.

Add cornstarch mixture, raisins, and almonds to oat bran. Mix
well. Spoon mixture into prepared pan. Let cool; then cover and
chill overnight.

To serve, invert mold onto a serving plate, remove plastic wrap,
and cut into 4 servings. Top with raspberry jam, if desired.

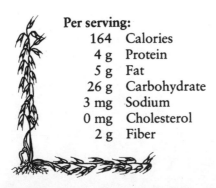

Per serving:

164	Calories
4 g	Protein
5 g	Fat
26 g	Carbohydrate
3 mg	Sodium
0 mg	Cholesterol
2 g	Fiber

Berries 'n Creme Oat Bran

*The addition of dry milk and vanilla makes this cereal
taste creamy and rich. It's a new and delicious way to
enjoy oat bran for breakfast.*

Make 2 servings

2   cups water
2/3 cup oat bran
1/2 cup nonfat dry milk
2   teaspoons vanilla extract
1   cup sliced, fresh strawberries (frozen, thawed berries can be
       used; look for the ones that are not packed in sugar)

Bring water to a boil over medium heat. Add oat bran, stirring
briskly with a fork or wire whisk to prevent lumps. Cook 1 to 2
minutes, stirring. Remove from heat.

Stir in dry milk and vanilla. Divide cereal evenly into 2 serving
bowls. Top with berries.

Sprinkle lightly with sugar or drizzle with honey to taste.

Per serving:
           209 Calories
          12 g Protein
           3 g Fat
          32 g Carbohydrate
          95 mg Sodium
           3 mg Cholesterol
           6 g Fiber

Carob Oat Bran

Add the dark, rich taste of carob to your breakfast for a real sweet treat. Available in many grocery stores and in most health food food stores, carob powder tastes somewhat like cocoa and, unlike cocoa, contains no caffeine.

Makes 2 servings

2   cups water
2/3   cup oat bran
1   tablespoon carob powder
       Brown sugar to taste

Bring water to a boil over medium heat. Add oat bran, stirring briskly with a fork or wire whisk to prevent mixture from forming lumps. Cook 1 to 2 minutes, stirring. Remove from heat and stir in carob powder.

Divide mixture into 2 serving bowls. Sprinkle with brown sugar to taste.

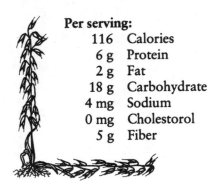

Per serving:
116 Calories
6 g Protein
2 g Fat
18 g Carbohydrate
4 mg Sodium
0 mg Cholestorol
5 g Fiber

Creamy Wheat Combo

*Cream of Wheat® and oat bran blend together so nicely
for a high-fiber breakfast that's smooth and mellow.*

Makes 4 servings

4   cups water
2/3   cup oat bran
1/3   cup quick Cream of Wheat®

Bring water to a boil over medium heat. Combine oat bran and
Cream of Wheat® and add to water, stirring briskly with a fork or
wire whisk to prevent mixture from forming lumps. Cook 2 to 3
minutes, stirring.

Serve hot, sprinkled with cinnamon, brown sugar, maple syrup,
or your favorite fruit topping.

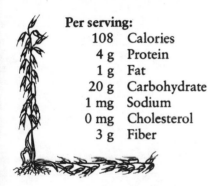

Per serving:
        108   Calories
        4 g   Protein
        1 g   Fat
        20 g Carbohydrate
        1 mg Sodium
        0 mg Cholesterol
        3 g   Fiber

Easy Duo

*If you want the concentrated fiber of oat bran but prefer
the coarser texture of traditional oatmeal, why not
combine the two?*

Makes 4 servings

3-1/2 cups water
2/3   cup rolled oats
2/3   cup oat bran

Bring water to a boil over medium heat. Combine rolled oats and
oat bran and add to water, stirring briskly with a fork or wire whisk
to prevent lumps from forming. Cook 5 minutes, stirring.

Serve hot, topped with cinnamon, maple syrup, or your favorite
fruit topping.

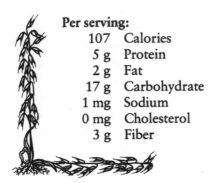

Per serving:

107	Calories
5 g	Protein
2 g	Fat
17 g	Carbohydrate
1 mg	Sodium
0 mg	Cholesterol
3 g	Fiber

Steel-Cut Oats 'n Apples

This hearty "stick-to-your-ribs" cereal can be eaten hot or cold. For variations, try a pear in place of the apple, or chopped dried apricots in place of the raisins.

Makes 4 servings

2-2/3	cups water
2/3	cup steel-cut oats
1	large, sweet apple, unpeeled, coarsely shredded (1 cup)
2	tablespoons brown sugar
1/2	teaspoon ground cinnamon
1	teaspoon vanilla extract
1/4	cup raisins

Bring water to a boil over medium heat. Add oats and cook 15 to 20 minutes, until oats are tender and water is absorbed. Remove from heat.

Stir in remaining ingredients.

Serve hot. Refrigerate any leftovers and serve them cold the following day or reheat them in a double boiler or microwave.

Per serving:

187	Calories
5 g	Protein
2 g	Fat
38 g	Carbohydrate
4 mg	Sodium
0 mg	Cholesterol
4 g	Fiber

Overnight Fruited Cereal

Put all the ingredients in the crockpot before you go to bed and enjoy a hearty breakfast that's ready when you are.

Makes 6 servings

1	cup steel-cut oats
1/3	cup raisins
1/3	cup chopped, mixed dried fruit*
1-1/2	teaspoons ground cinnamon
1/4	teaspoon ground allspice
1-1/2	teaspoons vanilla extract
1/4	teaspoon grated, fresh lemon peel
3-1/2	cups water

Combine all ingredients, *except* water in a large crockpot. Mix well. Add water, cover, and cook on low setting 6 to 8 hours or overnight.

If a thinner cereal is desired, stir a little water or milk into the finished cereal. Sweeten to taste.

*An easy way to chop dried fruit is to snip it with kitchen shears.

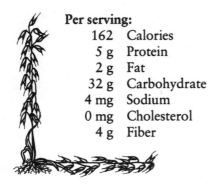

Per serving:

162	Calories
5 g	Protein
2 g	Fat
32 g	Carbohydrate
4 mg	Sodium
0 mg	Cholesterol
4 g	Fiber

Creamy Wheat and Oats

If you like cereal with a lot of texture, you'll love this delightful combination of cracked wheat and steel-cut oats. It's thick and bumpy, with lots of nutrition.

Makes 4 servings

2-1/3 cups water
1/3   cup steel-cut oats
1/2   cup cracked wheat (bulgur)
1/2   cup nonfat dry milk
1   teaspoon vanilla extract

Bring water to a boil in a medium saucepan over medium heat. Stir in oats and wheat. Cover, reduce heat to low, and simmer 15 minutes.

Remove from heat and stir in dry milk and vanilla.

Serve hot, sprinkled with brown sugar or drizzled lightly with honey or maple syrup.

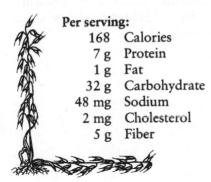

Per serving:

168	Calories
7 g	Protein
1 g	Fat
32 g	Carbohydrate
48 mg	Sodium
2 mg	Cholesterol
5 g	Fiber

Banana Mini-Pancakes

Drizzled lightly with maple syrup, these moist little pancakes make any breakfast a special occasion.

Makes 32 mini-pancakes

3/4	cup rolled oats
1/2	cup whole wheat flour
1/2	cup oat bran
2	teaspoons baking powder
1/2	teaspoon ground cinnamon
2	medium, ripe bananas, mashed (1 cup)
1-1/2	cups water
1	teaspoon vanilla extract

In a large bowl, combine dry ingredients, mixing well. Stir in remaining ingredients. Let stand 5 minutes.

Preheat a nonstick skillet or griddle over medium heat. Oil it lightly or spray with a nonstick cooking spray. Drop batter onto griddle, 1 tablespoonful at a time, making 32 small pancakes. Turn pancakes carefully when edges become dry. Flatten pancakes with a spatula and cook until golden brown on each side.

Per pancake:

26	Calories
1 g	Protein
0 g	Fat
5 g	Carbohydrate
27 mg	Sodium
0 mg	Cholesterol
1 g	Fiber

Blueberry Oat Cakes

The addition of oats and blueberries adds lots of fiber to these breakfast delights. Fluffy and light they're not, delicious and moist they are!

Makes 10 three-inch pancakes

3/4	cup rolled oats
3/4	cup whole wheat flour
1-1/2	teaspoons baking powder
1-1/2	tablespoons sugar
1	cup skim milk
2	egg whites
2	teaspoons vanilla extract
1	tablespoon vegetable oil
3/4	cup blueberries, fresh or frozen (if using frozen berries, thaw and drain before using)

In a large bowl, combine oats, flour, baking powder, and sugar. Mix well.

In a small bowl, whisk together milk, egg whites, vanilla, and oil. Add to dry mixture, mixing just until all ingredients are moistened. Fold in blueberries.

Preheat a nonstick skillet or griddle over medium heat. Oil it lightly or spray with a nonstick cooking spray. Drop batter onto griddle, using 2 tablespoonfuls for each pancake. Turn pancakes carefully when edges are dry and bottoms are lightly browned. Cook until golden brown on both sides.

Serve hot, drizzled with maple syrup, for best flavor.

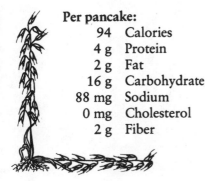

Per pancake:

94	Calories
4 g	Protein
2 g	Fat
16 g	Carbohydrate
88 mg	Sodium
0 mg	Cholesterol
2 g	Fiber

Cottage Cheese Pancakes

These sweet, cheesy pancakes are delicious plain or topped with fruit, jam, or maple syrup. They can make a simple brunch very elegant.

Makes 10 three-inch pancakes

1   cup low-fat cottage cheese
1   cup rolled oats
2   egg whites
2   tablespoons sugar
2   teaspoons vanilla extract
1/2   teaspoon ground cinnamon

In a blender container, combine all ingredients. Blend until cottage cheese is smooth (oats will be in small pieces).

Preheat a nonstick skillet or griddle over medium heat. Oil it lightly or spray with a nonstick cooking spray. Drop batter onto griddle, using 2 tablespoonfuls for each pancake. Turn pancakes carefully when edges are dry and bottoms are lightly browned. Cook until golden brown on both sides.

Serve hot.

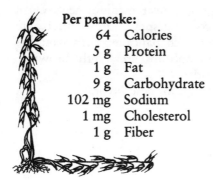

Per pancake:
            64   Calories
           5 g   Protein
           1 g   Fat
           9 g   Carbohydrate
        102 mg   Sodium
          1 mg   Cholesterol
           1 g   Fiber

Buckwheat–Oat Pancakes

Buckwheat lovers will adore the toasty flavor of these hearty pancakes.

Makes 15 four-inch pancakes

1	cup rolled oats
1/2	cup buckwheat flour
1/4	cup whole wheat flour
1	teaspoon baking powder
1/2	teaspoon baking soda
1	tablespoon sugar
1-1/2	cups skim milk
1	tablespoon lemon juice
2	teaspoons vanilla extract
2	egg whites
1	tablespoon vegetable oil

In a large bowl, combine oats, both types of flour, baking powder, baking soda, and sugar. Mix well.

In a small bowl, combine milk and lemon juice. Let stand 1 minute. Add remaining ingredients. Beat with a fork or wire whisk until blended. Add to dry mixture, mixing until all ingredients are moistened.

Let mixture stand 15 minutes.

Preheat a nonstick skillet or griddle over medium heat. Oil it lightly or spray with a nonstick cooking spray. Stir batter a few times, then drop onto griddle, using 2 tablespoonfuls for each pancake. Turn pancakes carefully when edges are dry and bottoms are lightly browned. Cook until golden brown on both sides.

Serve hot, drizzled with honey or maple syrup.

Per pancake:
65	Calories
3 g	Protein
1 g	Fat
10 g	Carbohydrate
76 mg	Sodium
0 mg	Cholesterol
1 g	Fiber*

*Fiber data is not available for buckwheat flour. Whole wheat flour was substituted in the analysis.

Applesauce Oat Pancakes

This breakfast favorite has a delightful combination of spices that will remind you of apple pie.

Makes 18 three-inch pancakes

1	cup rolled oats
3/4	cup whole wheat flour
1	tablespoon plus 1 teaspoon baking powder
1	teaspoon ground cinnamon
1/2	teaspoon ground nutmeg
1/8	teaspoon ground cloves
1	tablespoon sugar
3/4	cup applesauce (unsweetened)
2	egg whites
1	cup skim milk
2	tablespoons vegetable oil
1	teaspoon vanilla extract

In a large bowl, combine oats, flour, baking powder, and spices. Mix well.

In another bowl, combine remaining ingredients. Beat with a fork or wire whisk until blended. Add to dry mixture, mixing until all ingredients are moistened. Let stand 5 minutes, then mix again.

Preheat a nonstick skillet or griddle over medium heat. Oil it lightly or spray with a nonstick cooking spray. Drop batter onto griddle, using 2 tablespoonfuls for each pancake. Turn pancakes when edges are dry and bottoms are lightly browned. Cook until golden brown on both sides.

Note: If batter becomes too thick while standing, add a tablespoon or more of skim milk.

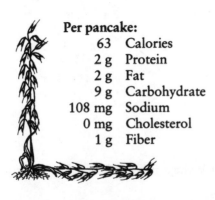

Per pancake:

63	Calories
2 g	Protein
2 g	Fat
9 g	Carbohydrate
108 mg	Sodium
0 mg	Cholesterol
1 g	Fiber

Overnight Cinnamon Waffles

Mix this easy batter up at night for a truly spectacular breakfast the next morning.

Makes 5 eight-inch waffles (20 sections)

4	cups rolled oats
1/4	cup whole wheat flour
1	tablespoon plus 1 teaspoon baking powder
2	teaspoons ground cinnamon
4	cups skim milk
3	tablespoons vegetable oil
2	teaspoons vanilla extract

In a large bowl, combine oats, flour, baking powder, and cinnamon. Mix well. Add remaining ingredients. Mix until all ingredients are moistened.

Cover and chill overnight.

To prepare:

Preheat a well-oiled waffle iron according to manufacturer's directions (or use a nonstick cooking spray).

Stir batter (it will be thick). Spoon batter onto center of hot iron, using 1 cup for each waffle. Close iron and cook 4 to 6 minutes. If using a cooking spray, be sure to spray before making each waffle.

Drizzle lightly with maple syrup or top with your favorite fruit topping.

Note: Leftover waffles can be refrigerated and later reheated in a toaster.

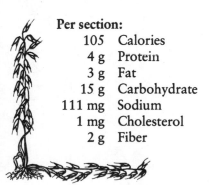

Per section:

105	Calories
4 g	Protein
3 g	Fat
15 g	Carbohydrate
111 mg	Sodium
1 mg	Cholesterol
2 g	Fiber

Oat Flour Pancakes

*These delightful pancakes are velvety-smooth with a
pleasing "oaty" flavor. Drizzle them with maple syrup
and enjoy!*

Makes 18 three-inch pancakes

1/2	cup oat flour (see directions on page 8)
1/2	cup whole wheat flour
2	teaspoons baking powder
1	tablespoon sugar
1	cup skim milk
1	tablespoon lemon juice
1	tablespoon vegetable oil
2	egg whites
1	teaspoon vanilla extract

In a medium bowl, combine both types of flour, baking powder,
and sugar. Mix well.

In a small bowl, combine milk and lemon juice. Let stand 1
minute. Add remaing ingredients. Beat with a fork or wire whisk
until blended. Add to dry mixture. Whisk until smooth.

Preheat a nonstick skillet or griddle over medium-low heat. Oil it
lightly or spray with a nonstick cooking spray. Drop batter onto
griddle, using 1-1/2 tablespoonfuls for each pancake. Turn pancakes
when edges are dry and bottoms are lightly browned. Cook until
golden brown on both sides.

Serve hot.

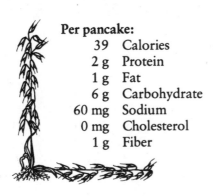

Per pancake:

39	Calories
2 g	Protein
1 g	Fat
6 g	Carbohydrate
60 mg	Sodium
0 mg	Cholesterol
1 g	Fiber

Soups

O*ats are a "natural" when* it comes to soup ingredients. Their chewy texture adds a thickness and richness to any type of broth. Soups made with oats are hearty and filling.

In the recipes that follow, I have combined oats with other high-fiber ingredients such as beans and vegetables. To make soups that are as low in fat as possible, these recipes contain no meat. Instead, I have relied on oats for thickness and spices for flavor. To keep the sodium content low, salt-free tomato products are used whenever possible, and most recipes read "salt and pepper to taste." This way you can add salt according to your own taste and dietary needs.

It seems that every soup I have ever tasted tastes better on the second day. So, my personal recommendation is to cook soup a day ahead, refrigerate overnight, and reheat the next day. Soups made with oats will become very thick when chilled, so reheat them first, and then add enough water until a desired texture is reached.

Here are some ideas to guide you in adding the fiber of oats to your favorite soups:

- When adding uncooked oats to soups, be sure to add enough water for the oats to absorb (see cooking directions on page 4).

- Be sure to cook soup long enough for oats to cook.

- Already cooked whole oats (groats) or steel-cut oats can be added to soups without the need for extra water.

- Use oats in combination with other high-fiber ingredients such as beans and vegetables.

- Use whole oats (groats) in place of, or in combination with, brown rice when rice is called for. (Brown rice is also a source of soluble fiber).

- Try adding uncooked rolled oats to tomato or chicken soup during the last 20 minutes of cooking.

- Remember that soups made with oats will tend to thicken as they stand, and more water may be needed.

"Oat-estroni" Soup

Similar to minestroni soup, but with oats instead of pasta,
this whole-meal soup is thick and rich and loaded with
oats and vegetables.

Makes 8 servings

2	tablespoons olive oil
1	cup chopped onions
2	cloves garlic, minced
1	cup chopped carrots, in 1/2-inch pieces
1	cup chopped celery, in 1/2-inch pieces
1	cup chopped celery leaves
2	1-pound cans salt-free (or regular) tomatoes, chopped, undrained
5-1/2	cups water
2/3	cup whole oats (groats)
1	15-ounce can kidney beans, rinsed and drained
1	bay leaf
1	teaspoon dried thyme
1-1/2	teaspoons dried basil
	Salt and pepper to taste

Heat oil in a large saucepan over medium heat. Add onions and garlic and cook 5 minutes. Add a small amount of water, if necessary, to prevent sticking.

Add remaining ingredients and bring mixture to a boil. Reduce heat to low, cover, and simmer 40 minutes.

Remove and discard bay leaf before serving.

Per serving:

172	Calories
7 g	Protein
5 g	Fat
27 g	Carbohydrate
221 mg	Sodium
0 g	Cholesterol
7 g	Fiber

Potato Oat Soup

This is one of our favorite cold-weather soups. It's hot, hearty, and very comforting.

Makes 8 servings

2	tablespoons vegetable oil
2	large potatoes (about 1 pound total), unpeeled, cut into 1/2-inch cubes
1	clove garlic, minced
1	cup chopped onions
1	cup coarsely shredded carrots
1/2	cup steel-cut oats
7	cups water
	Salt and pepper to taste

Heat oil in a large saucepan over medium heat. Add potatoes, garlic, onions, carrots and 1/2 cup of the water. Cover and cook 10 minutes, stirring occasionally. Add a little more water, if necessary, to prevent sticking.

Add oats, remaining water, salt, and pepper. Reduce heat to low, cover, and simmer 1 hour, stirring occasionally.

Per serving:

127	Calories
3 g	Protein
4 g	Fat
20 g	Carbohydrate
10 mg	Sodium
0 mg	Cholesterol
3 g	Fiber

Split Pea Soup

A soup so thick you can almost eat it with a fork; this is really a hearty dish.

Makes 8 servings

2	tablespoons olive oil
1	cup chopped onions
2	cloves garlic, minced
1	cup chopped carrots
8	cups water
1/2	cup steel-cut oats
2	cups dried split peas
1/4	teaspoon dried thyme
1	bay leaf
	Salt and pepper to taste

Heat oil in a large saucepan over medium heat. Add onions, garlic, and carrots. Cook, stirring frequently, until onions are tender, about 5 minutes.

Add remaining ingredients. Bring to a boil. Reduce heat to low, cover, and simmer 1 hour.

Remove and discard bay leaf before serving.

Per serving:

254	Calories
14 g	Protein
5 g	Fat
40 g	Carbohydrate
13 mg	Sodium
0 mg	Cholesterol
5 g	Fiber

Tomato Oatmeal Soup

Quick and easy, this soup proves that oatmeal isn't only for breakfast.

Makes 4 servings

2	tablespoons olive oil
1	cup chopped onions
2	cloves garlic, minced
1	1-pound can salt-free (or regular) tomatoes, chopped, undrained
3	cups water
1	packet instant low-sodium chicken-flavored broth mix (or vegetable broth mix)
	Salt and pepper to taste
1/2	cup rolled oats

Heat oil in a medium saucepan over medium heat. Add onions and garlic. Cook 5 to 10 minutes, until onions are tender. Add small amounts of water, if necessary, to prevent sticking.

Add remaining ingredients, *except* oats. Bring mixture to a boil. Stir in oats, reduce heat to low, cover, and simmer 20 minutes.

Per serving:

140	Calories
3 g	Protein
8 g	Fat
16 g	Carbohydrate
17 mg	Sodium
0 mg	Cholesterol
3 g	Fiber

Chili Oat Stew

*Whether you consider this mouth-watering dish a soup or
a stew, it's sure to become one of your favorite one-dish meals.*

Makes 8 servings

2	tablespoons olive oil
1	cup chopped onions
1	cup celery, sliced 1/2-inch thick
1	cup carrots, sliced 1/2-inch thick
2	cloves garlic, minced
1/2	cup water
1	8-ounce can salt-free (or regular) tomato sauce
1	1-pound can salt-free (or regular) tomatoes, chopped, undrained
1/2	cup steel-cut oats
5	cups water
2	medium potatoes (about 12 ounces total), unpeeled, coarsely shredded
1	teaspoon *each* dried basil and oregano
1	teaspoon chili powder
1/2	teaspoon ground cumin
1/2	teaspoon ground allspice
1	small bay leaf
	Salt to taste

Heat oil in a large saucepan over medium heat. Add onions, celery, carrots, garlic, and 1/2 cup water; cover and cook 15 minutes. Stir occasionally and add more water, if necessary, to prevent sticking.

Add remaining ingredients and bring to a boil. Cover, reduce heat to low, and simmer 45 minutes until vegetables are tender. Stir occasionally to keep oats from sticking.

Remove and discard bay leaf.

Per serving:

144	Calories
4 g	Protein
5 g	Fat
23 g	Carbohydrate
39 mg	Sodium
0 mg	Cholesterol
4 g	Fiber

Black Bean Soup

This thick, hearty soup combines the high fiber of beans and oats with just the right combination of spices. You'll love the results.

Makes 8 servings

2	cups dried black beans
	Water to cover beans
1	cup chopped onions
1	cup chopped carrots
1	8-ounce can salt-free (or regular) tomato sauce
1/2	teaspoon garlic powder
1-1/2	teaspoons dried oregano
2	bay leaves
7-1/2	cups water
	Salt and pepper to taste
1/2	cup steel-cut oats

Soak beans, using one of the following methods (this will reduce cooking time):

Overnight method—Place beans in a large pot and add enough water to cover beans by 2 inches. Soak overnight. Drain.

Quick soak—Place beans in a large pot and add enough water to cover beans by 2 inches. Bring to a boil over medium heat. Boil 2 minutes. Remove from heat, cover, and let stand 1 hour. Drain.

To prepare soup:

Place soaked beans in a large pot. Add remaining ingredients, *except* steel-cut oats. Bring to a boil over medium heat. Reduce heat to low, cover, and simmer 45 minutes.

Stir in oats and simmer, covered, 45 minutes more.

Remove and discard bay leaves before serving.

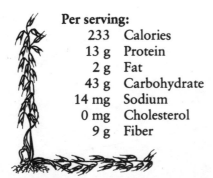

Per serving:

233	Calories
13 g	Protein
2 g	Fat
43 g	Carbohydrate
14 mg	Sodium
0 mg	Cholesterol
9 g	Fiber

Sweet 'n Sour Cabbage Soup

Slightly sweet and slightly sour, this delicately flavored soup goes well with a chunk of crusty rye bread.

Makes 10 servings

6	cups coarsely shredded cabbage
1	cup chopped onions
9	cups water
2	1-pound cans salt-free (or regular) tomatoes, chopped, undrained
1/3	cup lemon juice
1/4	cup sugar
1/4	teaspoon dried thyme
1	packet instant low-sodium chicken-flavored broth mix (or vegetable broth mix)
2/3	cup whole oats (groats)
	Salt and pepper to taste

Place cabbage and onions in a large soup pot with 2 cups of the water. Cover and cook over medium heat 15 minutes.

Add remaining ingredients. Bring mixture to a boil. Reduce heat to low, cover, and simmer 1 hour.

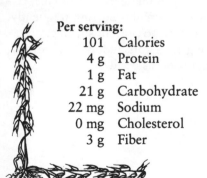

Per serving:

101	Calories
4 g	Protein
1 g	Fat
21 g	Carbohydrate
22 mg	Sodium
0 mg	Cholesterol
3 g	Fiber

Lentil Oat Soup

This soup is actually a meal in itself. Add a salad and a piece of whole-grain bread, and you have a delicious, nutritious dinner.

Makes 8 servings

2	tablespoons olive oil
1	cup chopped onions
1/2	cup chopped celery
1	cup chopped green pepper
2	cloves garlic, minced
2	1-pound cans salt-free (or regular) tomatoes, chopped, undrained
6	cups water
3/4	cup dry lentils, rinsed
3/4	cup whole oats (groats)
1/2	teaspoon dried rosemary, crumbled (crumble before measuring)
1	teaspoon dried oregano
1	teaspoon dried basil
	Salt and pepper to taste

Heat oil in a large saucepan over medium heat. Add onions, celery, green pepper, and garlic. Cook 5 minutes, stirring frequently. Add small amounts of water, if necessary, to prevent sticking.

Add remaining ingredients. Bring to a boil, reduce heat to low, cover, and simmer 45 minutes, stirring occasionally.

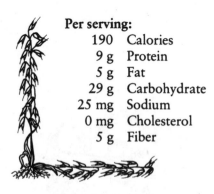

Per serving:

190	Calories
9 g	Protein
5 g	Fat
29 g	Carbohydrate
25 mg	Sodium
0 mg	Cholesterol
5 g	Fiber

Sweet Potato Soup

This is a very sweet-tasting soup with whole oats and chunks of vegetables throughout. Sweet potato lovers will be in heaven.

Makes 8 servings

2	tablespoons vegetable oil
1	cup chopped onions
1	cup chopped carrots
1/2	cup chopped celery
2	pounds sweet potatoes, peeled, cut into 1/2-inch pieces
1	tart, green apple, peeled, chopped (1 cup)
6-1/2	cups water
2/3	cup whole oats (groats)
2	small bay leaves
1/2	teaspoon dried thyme
1/4	teaspoon ground sage
	Salt and pepper to taste

Heat oil in a large saucepan over medium heat. Add onions, carrots, and celery. Cook until onions are tender, about 5 minutes.

Add remaining ingredients. Bring to a boil, cover, reduce heat to low, and simmer 45 minutes.

Skim 2 cups of vegetables off the top of the soup. (This will be easy because the oats will sink to the bottom). Place them in a blender container and blend until smooth, adding as much soup liquid as necessary to blend smoothly. Stir into soup and heat through.

Remove and discard bay leaves before serving.

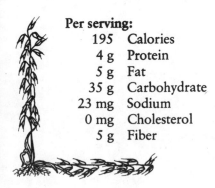

Per serving:

195	Calories
4 g	Protein
5 g	Fat
35 g	Carbohydrate
23 mg	Sodium
0 mg	Cholesterol
5 g	Fiber

Corn and Oat Chowder

Oats and corn combined make this a thick, nutritious soup that's perfect for starting any meal.

Makes 6 servings

2	tablespoons olive oil
1	clove garlic, minced
1/2	cup chopped onions
1	cup chopped celery
2-1/2	cups water
1	10-ounce package frozen corn, thawed
1/8	teaspoon pepper
	Salt to taste
1/4	teaspoon dried thyme
1/2	teaspoon dried basil
1	small bay leaf
2/3	cup rolled oats
2	cups skim milk

Heat oil in a large saucepan over medium heat. Add garlic, onions, and celery. Cook 10 minutes, until tender. Add small amounts of water, if necessary, to prevent sticking.

Add water, corn, and spices. Bring mixture to a boil. Stir in oats, cover, reduce heat to low, and simmer 10 minutes, stirring occasionally.

Stir in milk and heat through, stirring constantly. Do not boil.

Remove and discard bay leaf before serving.

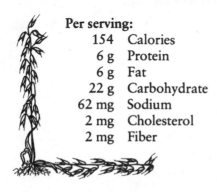

Per serving:

154	Calories
6 g	Protein
6 g	Fat
22 g	Carbohydrate
62 mg	Sodium
2 mg	Cholesterol
2 mg	Fiber

Entrées

O*ats and oat bran make* delicious, high-fiber coatings for chicken and fish, as well as nutritious additions to meatloaves and burgers. And, because meat products contain no fiber of their own, this is a way to add this much needed ingredient to what otherwise might be a no-fiber dish.

Many of us are modifying our intake of salt, and, for that reason, the recipes in this section often read "salt and pepper to taste". Go easy, and you will probably find that, with the use of spices and herbs, a lot of salt is not necessary.

To reduce the saturated fat content of these recipes, the vegetable oils that I use are either olive oil or canola oil. Any oil will work in a recipe, and the calorie count is about the same, but these two oils are high in monounsaturated fats, which many health professionals feel can help lower blood cholesterol levels.

Let the recipes in this section be your guide to adding the fiber of oats to your own favorite chicken or fish recipe.

Here are a few ideas to guide you:

- Use oat bran as a coating for chicken, either alone or in combination with wheat germ or bread crumbs.
- Use oat bran as a thickener for sauces.
- Add oat bran or rolled oats to meatloaves and burgers.
- Make fish cakes using oat bran as a binder in place of bread crumbs.
- Roll fish cakes and croquettes in oat bran for a coating with added texture and fiber.
- Make soups and stews with chicken or turkey, using whole oats in place of or in combination with rice and other whole grains.
- Sprinkle rolled oats over casseroles before baking.

Honey Orange Chicken

A delicious orange marinade, crunchy almonds, and
honey make this chicken dish really special.

Makes 4 servings

4	skinless, boneless chicken breast halves (1 pound total)
1/2	cup orange juice (unsweetened)
2	tablespoons dry sherry
1/4	cup oat bran
3	tablespoons finely chopped almonds
1	tablespoon vegetable oil
1	tablespoon plus 1 teaspoon honey
1	tablespoon cornstarch
1/4	cup water

Place chicken breasts in a shallow bowl.

Combine orange juice and sherry and pour over chicken. Marinate 5 to 6 hours or overnight in the refrigerator. Turn chicken several times while marinating.

When ready to cook:

Preheat oven to 350°.

Lightly oil a shallow baking pan or spray with a nonstick cooking spray.

In a small bowl, combine oat bran and almonds. Mix well. Remove chicken from marinade and pour marinade into a small saucepan. Dip each piece of chicken in crumbs, coating all sides. Place in prepared pan. Drizzle chicken with oil and 1 tablespoon of the honey.

Bake 45 minutes, uncovered.

When chicken is ready, add cornstarch, water, and remaining teaspoon of honey to marinade. Stir to dissolve cornstarch. Heat over medium heat, stirring frequently, until mixture comes to a boil. Cook, stirring, 2 to 3 minutes. Serve with chicken.

Per serving:

257	Calories
29 g	Protein
8 g	Fat
16 g	Carbohydrate
76 mg	Sodium
66 mg	Cholesterol
1 g	Fiber

Texas Baked Chicken

Marinated in barbecue sauce and rolled in a spicy oat bran topping, this chicken is really special.

Makes 4 servings

4   skinless, boneless chicken breast halves (1 pound total)

Marinade:

1   8-ounce can salt-free (or regular) tomato sauce
2   teaspoons prepared mustard
2   teaspoons vinegar
2   teaspoons reduced-sodium (or regular) soy sauce
1   tablespoon vegetable oil
1   tablespoon molasses
2   tablespoons grated onions
1/8   teaspoon garlic powder

Topping:

1/3   cup oat bran
1/3   cup wheat germ
1   teaspoon chili powder
2   teaspoons vegetable oil

Cut each chicken breast in half, lengthwise, making 8 long, thin pieces. Place chicken in a shallow baking pan. Combine marinade ingredients and pour over chicken. Refrigerate 5 or 6 hours or overnight, turning chicken several times.

When ready to cook:

Preheat oven to 350°.

Lightly oil a shallow baking pan or spray with a nonstick cooking spray.

In a small bowl, combine oat bran, wheat germ, and chili powder. Mix well. One at a time, lift chicken pieces out of sauce and dip in crumbs, coating all sides. Place in prepared pan. Drizzle with oil, using 1/4 teaspoon on each piece of chicken.

Bake 35 to 40 minutes, uncovered.

Place remaining marinade in a small saucepan. Add 1/4 cup of water. Heat and serve alongside chicken.

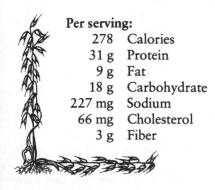

Per serving:

278	Calories
31 g	Protein
9 g	Fat
18 g	Carbohydrate
227 mg	Sodium
66 mg	Cholesterol
3 g	Fiber

Sesame Chicken

Herbs and sesame seeds add a delicious flavor to this tender baked chicken.

Makes 4 servings

4	skinless, boneless chicken breast halves (1 pound total)
1/4	cup oat bran
3	tablespoons wheat germ
2	tablespoons sesame seeds
1/4	teaspoon dried thyme
1/4	teaspoon garlic powder
1/4	teaspoon ground sage
1	teaspoon paprika
1/8	teaspoon pepper
	Salt to taste
4	teaspoons vegetable oil

Preheat oven to 350°.

Lightly oil a shallow baking pan or spray with a nonstick cooking spray.

In a small bowl, combine oat bran, wheat germ, sesame seeds, and spices. Mix well.

Dip each chicken breast in water, let the excess drip off, and then roll in crumb mixture. Place in prepared pan. Drizzle 1 teaspoon of oil over each piece of chicken. Bake 45 minutes, uncovered.

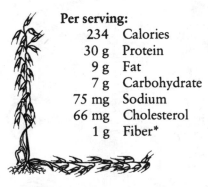

Per serving:

234	Calories
30 g	Protein
9 g	Fat
7 g	Carbohydrate
75 mg	Sodium
66 mg	Cholesterol
1 g	Fiber*

*Fiber is greater than number given. Data is not available for sesame seeds.

Pineapple Granola Chicken

A sweet, crunchy topping and slices of pineapple make this chicken dish refreshingly different.

Makes 4 servings

4   slices canned pineapple (unsweetened)
4   skinless, boneless chicken breast halves (1 pound total)
2/3 cup granola cereal (page 16), crushed*
2   teaspoons vegetable oil
2   teaspoons honey

Preheat oven to 350°.

Lightly oil a shallow baking pan or spray with a nonstick cooking spray.

Place pineapple rings in the bottom of prepared pan.

Roll each chicken breast in granola and place on a slice of pineapple. Sprinkle chicken with any remaining granola. Drizzle with oil and honey.

Bake 45 minutes, uncovered.

*An easy way to crush granola cereal is to place it in a plastic bag and crush it with a rolling pin. (Commercial granolas will also work, but read the labels carefully because many of them are loaded with fat.)

Per serving:
   275 Calories
   29 g Protein
    6 g Fat
   25 g Carbohydrate
  76 mg Sodium
  66 mg Cholesterol
    2 g Fiber

Chicken Oat Stew

*This hearty stew is loaded with chunks of chicken, whole
oats, and lima beans. It's even better the second day.*

Makes 6 servings

2	tablespoons vegetable oil
4	skinless, boneless chicken breast halves (1 pound total)
1	cup chopped onions
2	cloves garlic, minced
1	1-pound can salt-free (or regular) tomatoes, chopped, undrained
2	cups water
2/3	cup whole oats (groats)
1	10-ounce package frozen baby lima beans
2	small bay leaves
1/4	teaspoon dried rosemary (crumble before measuring)
1/8	teaspoon pepper
	Salt to taste
2	tablespoons oat flour (or cornstrach)
2	tablespoons water

Cut each chicken breast crosswise into 1/2-inch strips.

Heat oil in a large saucepan over medium heat. Add chicken, onions, and garlic. Cook until chicken is no longer pink, stirring frequently.

Add remaining ingredients, *except* oat flour and 2 tablespoons of
water. Bring to a boil, reduce heat to low, cover, and simmer 1
hour. Stir occasionally while cooking.

Stir water into oat flour until smooth. Add to stew. Cook, stirring
frequently, 5 minutes.

Remove and discard bay leaves before serving.

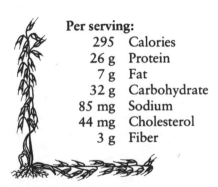

Per serving:

295	Calories
26 g	Protein
7 g	Fat
32 g	Carbohydrate
85 mg	Sodium
44 mg	Cholesterol
3 g	Fiber

Chicken Croquettes

*A wonderful use for leftover chicken, these tasty burgers
are delicious hot, and the leftovers make great
sandwiches.*

Makes 8 croquettes

Croquettes:

2	cups cooked, ground chicken (a food processor does a good job)
1/3	cup oat bran
1/2	cup plus 2 tablespoons skim milk
2	tablespoons grated onion
1/2	teaspoon poultry seasoning
1/8	teaspoon pepper
	Salt to taste

Topping:

3	tablespoons oat bran

In a large bowl, combine all croquette ingredients. Mix well.
Place in a shallow pan or bowl and chill several hours or overnight
until firm.

Shape mixture into 8 patties.

Dip each pattie in the oat bran topping.

Heat a nonstick skillet or griddle over medium heat. Oil it lightly
or spray with a nonstick cooking spray. Cook croquettes, turning
carefully, until brown on both sides.

Per croquette:

96	Calories
12 g	Protein
3 g	Fat
4 g	Carbohydrate
41 mg	Sodium
32 mg	Cholesterol
1 g	Fiber

Italian Cornish Hens

This delicately flavored dish makes a wonderful family meal as well as a party entrée you'll be proud to serve.

Makes 4 servings

2	1-1/4-pound Cornish hens
1/4	cup oat bran
1/4	cup wheat germ
2	tablespoons grated Parmesan cheese
1	teaspoon dried oregano
1/4	teaspoon pepper
1	tablespoon vegetable oil

Preheat over to 350°.

Lightly oil a shallow baking pan or spray with a nonstick cooking spray.

Split hens in half down the back. Remove skin.

Combine remaining ingredients, except vegetable oil, in a shallow pan. Roll hens in crumbs and place in prepared pan, ribs down. Drizzle with oil.

Bake, uncovered, 1 hour.

Per serving:

283	Calories
33 g	Protein
13 g	Fat
7 g	Carbohydrate
134 mg	Sodium
92 mg	Cholesterol
2 g	Fiber

Sweet 'n Sour Meatballs

These tasty meatballs are at their best when made ahead and reheated. Serve them over cooked whole oats, rice, or barley for a truly delicious dinner or serve them with toothpicks as an appetizer at your next party.

Makes 6 servings

1	pound ground turkey
1/4	cup finely chopped onions
2	tablespoons ketchup
1	cup cooked whole oats (groats) (see page 6 for cooking directions for whole oats)
	Salt and pepper to taste
1	cup chopped onions
1	8-ounce can salt-free (or regular) tomato sauce
1-1/2	cups water
3	tablespoons lemon juice
3	tablespoons sugar

In a large bowl, combine turkey, 1/4 cup onions, ketchup, oats, salt, and pepper. Mix well. Shape into meatballs, about 1-1/2 inches in diameter.

Place meatballs in a preheated nonstick sillet over medium heat. Brown on all sides.

While meatballs are browning, combine remaining ingredients in a 3-quart saucepan. Add browned meatballs and bring to a boil over medium heat. Reduce heat to low, cover, and simmer 30 minutes.

For best flavor, chill for several hours, or overnight, and reheat before serving. Add more lemon juice or sugar, according to taste.

Per serving:

211	Calories
16 g	Protein
8 g	Fat
20 g	Carbohydrate
130 mg	Sodium
48 mg	Cholesterol
2 g	Fiber

Turkey Cutlets Italiano

Tastily seasoned and elegant enough for your next dinner party, this dish also makes great "next -day" sandwiches. If turkey cutlets aren't available, have your grocer slice a turkey breast into thin slices.

Makes 6 servings

Cutlets:

1   pound turkey breast cutlets
3   tablespoons all-purpose flour
1   egg white
1/4   cup water
1/2   cup oat bran
1/4   cup wheat germ
1   teaspoon dried oregano
1/8   teaspoon garlic powder
2   teaspoons olive oil

Sauce:

1   8-ounce can salt-free (or regular) tomato sauce
1/4   teaspoon dried oregano
1/4   teaspoon dried basil
1/8   teaspoon garlic powder

Topping:

1/2   cup shredded part-skim Mozzarella cheese

Preheat oven to 375°.

Lightly oil a 10 × 15-inch baking pan or spray with a nonstick cooking spray.

Place flour in a small paper bag and put turkey cutlets in the bag, a few at a time. Close the bag tightly and turn it over gently several times to coat turkey.

In a shallow bowl, combine egg white and water.

In another shallow bowl, combine oat bran, wheat germ, oregano, and garlic powder.

Dip floured cutlets first in egg white mixture and then in oat bran, coating both sides. Place on prepared baking pan. Drizzle very lightly with oil, using about 1/8 teaspoon of oil on each cutlet.

Bake 20 minutes.

Combine sauce ingredients. Spread 1/3 of sauce in the bottom of an 8-inch square baking pan. Place turkey in overlapping layers on top of sauce. Top with remaining sauce. Sprinkle with cheese.

Cover with aluminum foil and bake 20 minutes.

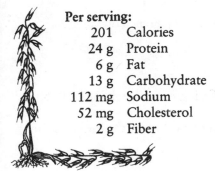

Per serving:
201	Calories
24 g	Protein
6 g	Fat
13 g	Carbohydrate
112 mg	Sodium
52 mg	Cholesterol
2 g	Fiber

French Turkey Burgers

*Served plain or on a bun, these burgers are a delicious,
lower-fat alternative to beef burgers.*

Makes 6 burgers

1	pound ground turkey
1/4	cup reduced-calorie sweet and spicy French dressing
1/2	cup oat bran
1	small onion, grated
	Salt and pepper to taste

Combine turkey with remaining ingredients, mixing well. Shape
into 6 burgers.

Cook in a preheated nonstick skillet or under the broiler, turning
several times, until done.

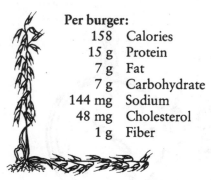

Per burger:

158	Calories
15 g	Protein
7 g	Fat
7 g	Carbohydrate
144 mg	Sodium
48 mg	Cholesterol
1 g	Fiber

Chili Turkey Burgers

*Green chilies add flavor and zest, and oat bran adds fiber
to these tender, moist burgers.*

Makes 6 burgers

1	pound ground turkey
1	8-ounce can salt-free (or regular) tomato sauce
1/2	cup oat bran
1/3	cup finely chopped onions
1	4-ounce can chopped green chilies, drained
1/2	teaspoon dried oregano
1/4	teaspoon garlic powder
	Salt and pepper to taste

In a large bowl, combine turkey, *half* of the tomato sauce, and remaining ingredients. Mix well. Shape into 6 burgers.

Cook in a preheated nonstick skillet or under the broiler, turning
several times, until done.

Add a dash *each* of dried basil, dried oregano, and garlic powder
to remaining tomato sauce. Spoon over burgers toward the end of
cooking time.

Per burger:

167	Calories
16 g	Protein
8 g	Fat
9 g	Carbohydrate
184 mg	Sodium
48 mg	Cholesterol
2 g	Fiber

Chili Turkey Loaf

Ground turkey is leaner than ground beef and makes a great meatloaf. You'll love the flavor and texture of this one.

Makes 6 servings

1	pound ground turkey
2/3	cup rolled oats
1/2	cup finely chopped onions
1/2	cup finely chopped green pepper
1/3	cup bottled chili sauce
1/4	cup water

Preheat oven to 350°.

Lightly oil a shallow baking pan or spray with a nonstick cooking spray.

Combine all ingredients in a large bowl and mix well. Shape into a loaf in prepared pan.

Bake, uncovered, 1 hour.

Per seving:

174	Calories
16 g	Protein
7 g	Fat
11 g	Carbohydrate
262 mg	Sodium
48 mg	Cholesterol
1 g	Fiber

Tuna Loaf Italiano

Serve this tasty loaf hot the first day and cold, in sandwiches, the next day. It's a real winner.

Makes 6 servings

2	6½-ounce cans water-pack tuna, drained
3/4	cup rolled oats
1/4	cup finely shredded carrots
1/2	cup finely chopped onions
1	8-ounce can salt-free (or regular) tomato sauce
1	tablespoon vegetable oil
1	teaspoon dried basil
1/2	teaspoon dried oregano
1/4	teaspoon garlic powder

Preheat oven to 350°.

Lightly oil a 4 × 8-inch loaf pan or spray with a nonstick cooking spray.

In a large bowl, combine all ingredients. Mix well. Press mixture firmly into prepared pan.

Bake 45 minutes.

Let cool in pan 5 minutes. Then invert onto a serving plate.

Per serving:

152	Calories
19 g	Protein
3 g	Fat
11 g	Carbohydrate
206 mg	Sodium
23 mg	Cholesterol
2 g	Fiber

Salmon Croquettes

These delicious patties make great sandwiches. Try them hot or cold, with a little ketchup, on bread or crackers.

Makes 8 croquettes

1/4	cup oat bran
1/4	cup skim milk
2	6½-ounce cans skinless, boneless salmon, drained
2	egg whites
2	teaspoons lemon juice
2	teaspoons prepared mustard
2	tablespoons ketchup
2	tablespoons grated onion
	Salt and pepper to taste

In a large bowl, combine all ingredients, mixing well. Let stand 10 minutes.

Shape mixture into eight 3-inch patties. (Mixture will be loose, but this will make tender, moist croquettes). Preheat a nonstick skillet or griddle over medium heat. Oil it lightly or spray with a nonstick cooking spray. Cook croquettes until brown on both sides, turning carefully.

Serve hot or cold.

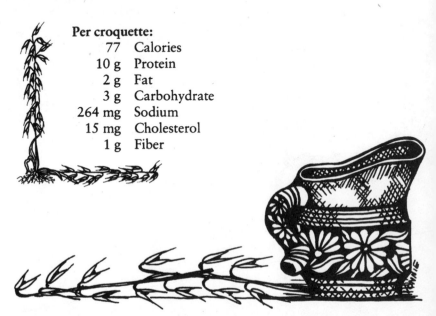

Per croquette:

77	Calories
10 g	Protein
2 g	Fat
3 g	Carbohydrate
264 mg	Sodium
15 mg	Cholesterol
1 g	Fiber

French Fish Fillets

So easy and yet so elegant, these fillets are a real winner.

Makes 4 servings

1	pound thickly-cut fish fillets (such as scrod or orange roughy), cut into 4-inch pieces
1/2	cup reduced-calorie sweet and spicy French dressing
1	tablespoon lemon juice
1/4	cup oat bran
1/4	cup dry bread crumbs
1	teaspoon paprika
4	teaspoons vegetable oil

In a large bowl, combine dressing and lemon juice. Add fish, mixing gently to coat each piece. Marinate several hours in the refrigerator, mixing occasionally.

To cook:

Preheat oven to 350°.

Lightly oil a shallow baking pan or spray with a nonstick cooking spray.

In a small bowl, combine oat bran, bread crumbs, and paprika. Mix well.

Roll each piece of fish in crumbs and place in prepared pan. Drizzle oil over fillets.

Bake 35 to 40 minutes, uncovered, until fish flakes easily.

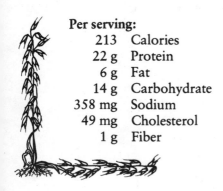

Per serving:

213	Calories
22 g	Protein
6 g	Fat
14 g	Carbohydrate
358 mg	Sodium
49 mg	Cholesterol
1 g	Fiber

Dijon Fish Bits

Cutting the fish fillets into small pieces makes a lot more surfaces to coat with the tangy Dijon mustard and oat bran.

Makes 4 servings

1	pound thickly-cut fish fillets (such as scrod or orange roughy)
3	tablespoons reduced-calorie mayonnaise
4-1/2	teaspoons Dijon mustard
1/8	teaspoon garlic powder
1/3	cup oat bran
3	tablespoons wheat germ

Preheat oven to 350°.

Lightly oil a shallow baking pan or spray with a nonstick cooking spray.

Cut fish into 1 × 3-inch pieces. Place on a flat plate or piece of wax paper.

In a small bowl or custard cup, combine mayonnaise, mustard, and garlic powder. Using *half* of the mayonnaise mixture, paint the top and sides of each piece of fish.

In another bowl, combine oat bran and wheat germ. Sprinkle evenly over fillets, using *half* of the oat bran mixture. Carefully turn fillets over. Brush with remaining mayonnaise. Sprinkle with remaining crumbs.

Place fish in prepared pan. Let stand 15 minutes at room temperature so crumbs can absorb some of the mayonnaise.

Bake 25 minutes, uncovered.

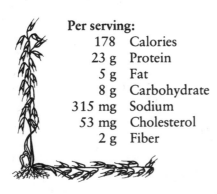

Per serving:

178	Calories
23 g	Protein
5 g	Fat
8 g	Carbohydrate
315 mg	Sodium
53 mg	Cholesterol
2 g	Fiber

Company Fish Casserole

Besides being served as a casserole, this marvelous-tasting dish can also be baked and served in individual ramekins.

Makes 4 servings

1/2	cup skim milk
2	tablespoons reduced-calorie mayonnaise
1	tablespoon lemon juice
1	teaspoon Dijon mustard
1	tablespoon dry sherry
1/8	teaspoon pepper
1/4	cup oat bran
1	egg white
12	ounces cooked fish, flaked

Topping:

1	tablespoon oat bran
1	tablespoon wheat germ
1/2	teaspoon paprika
1-1/2	teaspoons vegetable oil

Preheat oven to 375°.

Lightly oil a 1-quart baking dish or spray with a nonstick cooking spray.

In a large bowl, combine milk, mayonnaise, lemon juice, mustard, sherry, pepper, and oat bran. Let stand 10 minutes. Add egg white. Beat with a fork or wire whisk until smooth. Add fish. Mix gently until well blended.

Place mixture in prepared dish. Combine remaining oat bran, wheat germ, and paprika. Sprinkle evenly over fish. Drizzle with oil.

Bake 20 minutes, uncovered.

For a crisp topping, place finished casserole under the broiler for 3 minutes, until brown.

Per serving:

187	Calories
24 g	Protein
6 g	Fat
8 g	Carbohydrate
213 mg	Sodium
61 mg	Cholesterol
1 g	Fiber

Fish Cakes

Oat bran makes a wonderful binder to hold the fish together in these delicious "mock crab cakes".

Makes 10 cakes

1	pound cooked fish, flaked (use any non-oily fish, such as flounder, sole, or orange roughy)*
1/4	cup oat bran
1	teaspoon seafood seasoning
1	tablespoon dried parsley flakes
2	teaspoons baking powder
2	tablespoons reduced-calorie mayonnaise
2	egg whites
1/4	cup skim milk
	Salt to taste

In a large bowl, combine all ingredients. Mix well. Shape into 10 patties. Place in refrigerator and chill 1 hour or more.

Preheat a nonstick skillet or griddle over medium heat. Oil it lightly or spray with a nonstick cooking spray. Cook fish cakes until lightly browned on both sides, turning carefully several times.

*One and one-quarter pounds of raw fish will yield approximately 1 pound of cooked fish.

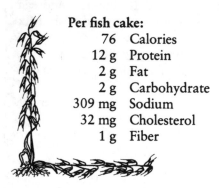

Per fish cake:

76	Calories
12 g	Protein
2 g	Fat
2 g	Carbohydrate
309 mg	Sodium
32 mg	Cholesterol
1 g	Fiber

Meatless Entrées

Being high in protein and vitamins, oats make a perfect addition to meatless entrées. They combine well with vegetables and beans and are easy to prepare. The wonderful "oaty" flavor is bland enough to take on the taste of whatever spices you use, yet substantial enough to "hold its own". And, the unique texture helps bind the other ingredients together, without the need for a lot of eggs or other high-fat ingredients.

Meatless burgers and loaves are as nutritious and filling as their more traditional counterparts. The recipes in this section are very low in cholesterol. Wherever cheese is called for, I have used only the low-fat varieties. For oil, I always use either olive oil or canola oil, both of which are recommended by health professionals for possibly lowering blood cholesterol levels. As in the previous sections, most of the recipes read "salt and pepper to taste". Remember to go easy and taste before you add salt. There are a lot of different spices in these recipes, and you will probably find that salt is not necessary.

For high-fiber meatless alternatives to dinner, try these suggestions:

- Make meatless burgers by mashing cooked beans, such as kidney or pinto beans, with cooked whole oats (groats).

- For meatless croquettes, chill leftover oatmeal in a shallow pan, cut it into squares, and brown on both sides.

- Add oat bran and whole wheat flour to pizza crust and top with low-fat cheese and vegetables.

- Cook beans, oats, and vegetables in a crockpot for a really easy and filling dinner.

- Combine oat bran with cornmeal for a doubly nutritious polenta.

- Add rolled oats or oat bran to mashed tofu for great burgers and meatless loaves.

- Make hearty meatless stews with beans, oats, and vegetables in salt-free tomato broth.

Veggie Pan Pizza

This delicious version of the all-American favorite has lots of added nutrition.

Makes 8 slices

Dough:

1/2	cup whole wheat flour
1/2	cup all-purpose flour
1/2	cup oat bran
1	teaspoon baking powder
1/2	teaspoon salt
3/4	cup plus 1 tablespoon water

Sauce:

1/2	cup salt-free (or regular) tomato sauce
1/8	teaspoon *each* dried oregano and basil
	Dash garlic powder

Topping:

2/3	cup shredded part-skim Mozzarella cheese
3	tablespoons *each* finely chopped onions, mushrooms, and green pepper

Preheat oven to 400°. Lightly oil a 10-inch heavy cast iron skillet or spray with a nonstick cooking spray.

To prepare crust:

In a large bowl, combine dry ingredients, mixing well. Add water. Stir until all ingredients are moistened. Place dough in prepared skillet. Press in pan, wetting your hands slightly to avoid sticking.

Bake 10 minutes. Remove pan from oven.

To assemble pizza:

Combine tomato sauce and spices. Spread evenly over dough, staying 1/2-inch away from edge of pan.

Sprinkle cheese and then vegetables evenly over sauce.

Bake 15 minutes. Serve right from skillet.

Per slice:

106	Calories
5 g	Protein
2 g	Fat
16 g	Carbohydrate
238 mg	Sodium
6 mg	Cholesterol
2 g	Fiber

Mexicali Squares

Mexican-flavored beans on an oat and cornbread crust make an unforgettable dinner.

Makes 6 servings

Topping:
2	tablespoons olive oil
1	clove garlic, minced
1	cup chopped onions
1	cup chopped green pepper
1-1/3	cups cooked kidney beans
1	8-ounce can salt-free (or regular) tomato sauce
1	teaspoon dried oregano
1	teaspoon ground cumin
1	teaspoon chili powder

Crust:
1/2	cup oat bran
1/2	cup yellow cornmeal
1	teaspoon baking powder
2	egg whites
1/2	cup skim milk
2	tablespoons olive oil
1	cup canned corn, drained

Preheat oven to 350°.

Lightly oil an 8-inch square baking pan or spray with a nonstick cooking spray.

To prepare topping:

Heat oil in a large nonstick skillet over medium heat. Add garlic, onions and green pepper. Cook 10 minutes, until onions are tender and start to brown. Remove from heat and stir in remaining topping ingredients. Set aside.

To prepare crust:

In a small bowl, combine oat bran, cornmeal, and baking powder. Mix well.

In another bowl, combine egg whites, milk, and oil. Beat with a fork or wire whisk until blended. Add to oat bran mixture, mixing until all ingredients are moistened. Stir in corn.

Spread crust mixture evenly in prepared baking pan (mixture will be loose). Spoon filling evenly over crust.

Bake 35 minutes, uncovered.

Cut into squares to serve.

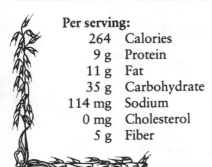

Per serving:

264	Calories
9 g	Protein
11 g	Fat
35 g	Carbohydrate
114 mg	Sodium
0 mg	Cholesterol
5 g	Fiber

Italian Polenta

*The winning combination of cornmeal and oat bran,
topped with sauce and cheese, makes an easy, nutritious,
and inexpensive pizza-like dinner.*

Polenta: *Makes 6 servings*

3   cups water
1/2   cup *each* oat bran and yellow cornmeal
1   tablespoon grated Parmesan cheese

Sauce:

1   8-ounce can salt-free (or regular) tomato sauce
1/4   teaspoon *each* dried basil and oregano
1/8   teaspoon garlic powder

Topping:

3   ounces shredded part-skim Mozzarella cheese

Lightly oil an 8-inch square baking pan or spray with a nonstick cooking spray.

Bring water to a boil in a small saucepan over medium heat (use a nonstick saucepan if available). Combine oat bran and cornmeal. Add to boiling water, stirring briskly with a fork or wire whisk to prevent lumps. Reduce heat to low and simmer 30 minutes, stirring frequently, until mixture is very thick. Spread in prepared pan. Sprinkle evenly with Parmesan cheese.

Cool slightly; then cover and chill several hours or overnight.

To bake:

Remove polenta from refrigerator 1 hour before baking.

Preheat oven to 400°. Bake 15 minutes.

While polenta is baking, prepare sauce by combining all ingredients in a small bowl.

Remove polenta from oven and turn on broiler. Spread sauce evenly over top and sprinkle with Mozzarella cheese.

Broil 2 to 3 minutes until cheese is melted.

Cut into squares to serve.

Per serving:

123	Calories
7 g	Protein
3 g	Fat
16 g	Carbohydrate
90 mg	Sodium
9 mg	Cholesterol
2 g	Fiber

Oat-Stuffed Peppers

*The oats, beans, and cheese make this old-time favorite a
real gourmet treat—without a lot of fuss.*

Makes 4 servings

4	large green peppers
2	cups cooked whole oats (groats) (see cooking directions on page 6)
1	cup cooked kidney beans
1/2	cup shredded low-fat Cheddar cheese
1	1-pound can salt-free (or regular) tomatoes, drained, chopped (reserve juice)
1/4	cup juice from tomatoes
1/2	teaspoon dried oregano
1/4	teaspoon dried basil
	Dash garlic powder
	Salt and pepper to taste
4	teaspoons vegetable oil

Preheat oven to 375°.

Lightly oil a shallow baking pan or spray with a nonstick cooking spray.

Slice off the top of each pepper and remove seeds. Place peppers in a pot of boiling water. Boil 5 minutes. Remove peppers from water and drain, upside-down, on paper towels.

In a large bowl, combine remaining ingredients, *except* oil. Mix well.

Fill peppers with oat mixture. Drizzle 1 teaspoon of oil over the top of each pepper.

Place peppers in prepared pan.

Bake 20 to 25 minutes, uncovered, until heated through.

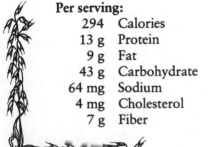

Per serving:

294	Calories
13 g	Protein
9 g	Fat
43 g	Carbohydrate
64 mg	Sodium
4 mg	Cholesterol
7 g	Fiber

Savory Oat Burgers

*These deliciously herbed burgers taste great in a whole
wheat pita or on a bun, with your favorite burger
toppings.*

Makes 6 burgers

2	tablespoons vegetable oil
1	medium onion, chopped
1	clove garlic, minced
2	cups rolled oats
1/4	cup wheat germ
1/4	teaspoon ground sage
1/4	teaspoon dried thyme
1/2	teaspoon dried oregano
	Pepper to taste
1-1/3	cups water
1	tablespoon reduced-sodium (or regular) soy sauce

Heat oil in a nonstick skillet over medium heat. Add onion and
garlic. Cook 5 to 10 minutes, until onion is tender and starts to
brown.

In a large bowl, combine onion with remaining ingredients and
mix well. Let stand 10 minutes.

While mixture is standing, preheat oven to 350°.

Lightly oil a baking sheet or spray with a nonstick cooking spray.

Drop mixture by 1/3 cupfuls onto prepared sheet. Flatten each
burger to 1/2-inch thick.

Bake 30 minutes.

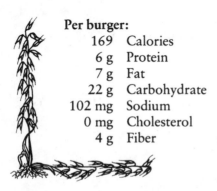

Per burger:

169	Calories
6 g	Protein
7 g	Fat
22 g	Carbohydrate
102 mg	Sodium
0 mg	Cholesterol
4 g	Fiber

Bean and Oat Burgers

*Try these wonderful, meatless burgers on whole grain
buns with your favorite burger "fixins". All the flavor is
there without the fat.*

Makes 6 burgers

2   cups cooked whole oats (groats) (see cooking directions on
             page 6)
1-1/2   cups cooked kidney beans
2   tablespoons minced onion flakes
2   tablespoons reduced-sodium (or regular) soy sauce
1/8   teaspoon dried thyme
1/2   teaspoon ground sage
1/4   teaspoon garlic powder

Combine all ingredients in a food processor or grinder. Process
until mixture holds together. Shape into 6 burgers.

Preheat a nonstick skillet or griddle over medium heat. Oil it
lightly or spray with a nonstick cooking spray.

Cook burgers until brown on both sides, turning carefully.

Per burger:
       139 Calories
        7 g Protein
        1 g Fat
       25 g Carbohydrate
      202 mg Sodium
        0 mg Cholesterol
        4 g Fiber

Zesty Bean Bake

Like oats, beans are a good source of soluble fiber. This main dish contains oats and beans in a slightly sweet, slightly sour sauce that makes a hit every time.

Makes 6 servings

2	tablespoons olive oil
1	clove garlic, minced
1	cup *each* chopped onions and red pepper
1	8-ounce can salt-free (or regular) tomato sauce
1/4	cup water
1/3	cup apple juice
1	tablespoon firmly packed brown sugar
1	tablespoon vinegar
1	teaspoon prepared mustard
2	tablespoons oat bran
1	1-pound can Great Northern beans, or butter beans, rinsed and drained
1	1-pound can kidney beans, rinsed and drained
1/4	cup rolled oats

Heat oil in large nonstick skillet over medium heat. Add garlic, onions, and peppers. Cook 5 to 10 minutes, until tender. Remove from heat.

Preheat oven to 350°.

Lightly oil a deep casserole or spray with a nonstick cooking spray.

In a large bowl, combine onion mixture with remaining ingredients, *except* rolled oats. Mix well. Place in prepared casserole and sprinkle top with rolled oats.

Bake 30 minutes, covered. Uncover; bake 30 minutes more.

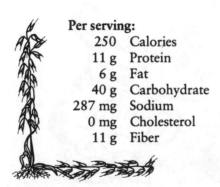

Per serving:

250	Calories
11 g	Protein
6 g	Fat
40 g	Carbohydrate
287 mg	Sodium
0 mg	Cholesterol
11 g	Fiber

Cheddar Beans and Oats

This casserole is so thick and delicious, they'll never believe it's good for them!

Makes 6 servings

2	tablespoons olive oil
2	cloves garlic, minced
1	cup chopped onions
1	cup chopped green pepper
1	cup sliced mushrooms
1	8-ounce can salt-free (or regular) tomato sauce
1	1-pound can kidney beans, rinsed and drained
1	teaspoon dried basil
1	teaspoon dried oregano
1/4	teaspoon dried thyme
1/2	teaspoon chili powder
3	ounces shredded low-fat Cheddar cheese
2	cups cooked whole oats (groats) (see cooking directions on page 6)

Preheat oven to 350°.

Heat oil in a large nonstick skillet over medium heat. Add garlic, onions, and green pepper. Cook 5 minutes, until tender, stirring frequently and adding small amounts of water, if necessary, to prevent drying.

Add mushrooms. Cook 5 minutes, stirring frequently.

Remove from heat and add remaining ingredients, mixing well. Spoon mixture into a lightly oiled casserole or one that has been sprayed with a nonstick cooking spray.

Bake, covered, 40 minutes.

Per serving:

280	Calories
14 g	Protein
9 g	Fat
40 g	Carbohydrate
58 mg	Sodium
4 mg	Cholesterol
6 g	Fiber

Bean Loaf

*Oats, beans, and carrots make this deliciously spiced loaf
a real high-fiber meal. Try it hot for dinner and have the
leftovers in a sandwich the next day.*

Makes 6 servings

1	cup rolled oats
3/4	cup water
1	1-pound can Great Northern beans, or butter beans, rinsed and drained
1	cup finely shredded carrots
1/2	cup finely chopped onions
2	tablespoons oat bran
1	egg white
1/8	teaspoon garlic powder
1/8	teaspoon pepper
1/4	teaspoon *each* dried oregano, basil and thyme
1/4	teaspoon ground sage
	Salt to taste

Preheat oven to 350°.

Lightly oil a 4 × 8-inch loaf pan or spray with a nonstick cooking spray.

Place oats and water in a small bowl and let stand 15 minutes.

While oats are standing, place beans in a large bowl. Mash with a fork or potato masher. Add remaining ingredients. Mix well with a fork, making sure that spices are evenly distributed.

Add oats to bean mixture. Mix well. Press firmly into prepared pan.

Bake 1 hour and 15 minutes.

Invert onto a serving plate. Let stand 5 minutes before slicing.

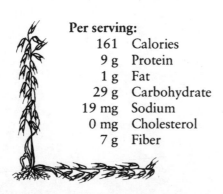

Per serving:

161	Calories
9 g	Protein
1 g	Fat
29 g	Carbohydrate
19 mg	Sodium
0 mg	Cholesterol
7 g	Fiber

Spiced Cheese and Oat Loaf

An unusual blend of spices makes this loaf a very tasty dish. Add a salad and a green vegetable and your meal is complete. The leftovers also make delicious sandwiches.

Makes 6 servings

2	cups rolled oats
2	tablespoons minced onion flakes
1/4	teaspoon garlic powder
1/4	teaspoon ground sage
1/8	teaspoon dried thyme
1/8	teaspoon ground allspice
	Salt and pepper to taste
2	cups low-fat cottage cheese
4	egg whites

Preheat oven to 350°.

Lightly oil a 4 x 8-inch loaf pan or spray with a nonstick cooking spray.

In a large bowl, combine dry ingredients. Mix well.

In another bowl, combine cottage cheese and egg whites. Beat with a fork or wire whisk until blended. Add to dry mixture, mixing until all ingredients are moistened.

Press mixture firmly into prepared pan.

Cover pan with aluminum foil and bake 25 minutes. Uncover and continue baking 25 minutes more.

Let stand 3 to 5 minutes, then invert onto a serving plate.

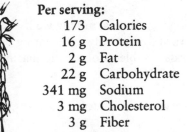

Per serving:

173	Calories
16 g	Protein
2 g	Fat
22 g	Carbohydrate
341 mg	Sodium
3 mg	Cholesterol
3 g	Fiber

Oriental Sesame Tofu

The tofu is marinated in an Oriental sauce and then rolled in oat bran and sesame seeds in this unusual and delicious recipe.

Makes 4 servings

1   pound medium or firm tofu, sliced 1/2-inch thick

Marinade:
3   tablespoons vegetable oil
3   tablespoons red wine vinegar
3   tablespoons reduced-sodium (or regular) soy sauce
2/3   cup water
2   teaspoons dried oregano
1/4   teaspoon garlic powder
1/8   teaspoon pepper
2   teaspoons sugar

Topping:
1/4   cup oat bran
2   tablespoons sesame seeds
2   tablespoons wheat germ

Combine marinade ingredients in a shallow baking pan. Add tofu and marinate in the refrigerator 4 to 5 hours, or longer. Turn tofu several times while marinating.

When ready to prepare:
Preheat oven to 375°.

Lightly oil a shallow baking pan or spray with a nonstick cooking spray.

In a small bowl, combine topping ingredients, mixing well.

Dip each tofu slice in topping, turning carefully and coating both sides. Place in prepared pan. Drizzle 1 tablespoon of the marinade over each slice.

Bake 25 minutes, uncovered.

Heat remaining marinade and serve alongside tofu.

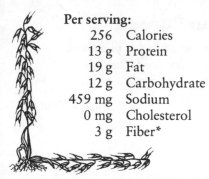

Per serving:

256	Calories
13 g	Protein
19 g	Fat
12 g	Carbohydrate
459 mg	Sodium
0 mg	Cholesterol
3 g	Fiber*

*Fiber is greater than number given. Data is not available for sesame seeds.

Mexican Tofu Burgers

*For a real Mexican treat, serve these burgers in a whole
wheat pita, topped with tomato, shredded lettuce,
shredded low-fat Cheddar cheese, and bottled salsa.*

Makes 6 burgers

1	pound medium tofu
1/2	cup oat bran
1/2	teaspoon ground cumin
1	teaspoon chili powder (or more, to taste)
1/4	teaspoon garlic powder
2	tablespoons minced onion flakes
	Salt and pepper to taste

Preheat a nonstick skillet or griddle over medium heat.

Oil it lightly or spray with a nonstick cooking spray.

Place tofu in a large bowl and mash well with a fork. Add remaining ingredients, mixing well. Shape mixture into 6 burgers and place on preheated skillet. Cook until burgers are brown on both sides, turning carefully.

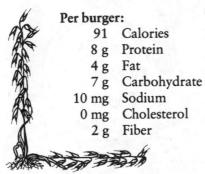

Per burger:

91	Calories
8 g	Protein
4 g	Fat
7 g	Carbohydrate
10 mg	Sodium
0 mg	Cholesterol
2 g	Fiber

Tofu Oat Loaf

One of the beauties of tofu is that it's very bland and takes on the flavor of whatever you mix with it—in this case Italian spices for flavor, and oats for texture and fiber.

Makes 6 servings

1	pound medium tofu
2	cups bottled marinara sauce, or spaghetti sauce
1/3	cup finely chopped onions
1/2	cup finely chopped green pepper
1/4	teaspoon garlic powder
1	teaspoon dried oregano
1/2	teaspoon dried basil
1/8	teaspoon pepper
1	cup rolled oats
1/4	cup wheat germ

Preheat oven to 350°.

Lightly oil a 4 x 8-inch loaf pan or spray with a nonstick cooking spray.

Rinse tofu, drain it slightly, and place it in a large bowl with 1/3 cup of the marinara sauce. Add onions, green pepper, and spices and mash well with a fork.

Add oats and wheat germ. Mix until well blended.

Press mixture firmly into prepared pan.

Bake 45 minutes.

While loaf is baking, heat remaining marinara sauce in a small saucepan.

Let loaf stand 5 minutes, then invert onto a serving plate. Serve with sauce.

Per serving:

191	Calories
11 g	Protein
8 g	Fat
23 g	Carbohydrate
531 mg	Sodium
0 mg	Cholesterol
3 g	Fiber

Vegetables and
Side Dishes

Finding interesting ways to add oats to vegetables was challenging and fun. Oat bran makes a wonderful coating for oven-fried vegetables, as well as a nutritious thickener for vegetable casseroles and puddings.

As for other side dishes, oats are a "natural". Any of your favorite spices can be added to whole oats (groats) while cooking, making the possible combinations limited only by your imagination. You can serve oats topped with your favorite spaghetti sauce or piled high with stir-fried vegetables. The possibilities are endless.

For added nutrition, try using whole oats in combination with other whole grains such as brown rice, barley, rye, or wheat berries. If you can't find these grains in your grocery store, they're well worth a trip to the nearest health food store.

Here are some tips to help get you started in adding the nutrition of oats to your vegetable recipes and side dishes:

- Use oat bran as a thickener in vegetable casseroles.
- Sprinkle casseroles with rolled oats before baking.
- Add your favorite regional flavor to cooked whole oats, such as basil and oregano for Italian flavor, curry powder for Indian flavor, or chili powder for Mexican flavor.
- Top cooked whole oats with melted low-fat Cheddar cheese for a side dish that closely resembles macaroni and cheese.
- Combine oat bran with wheat germ or bread crumbs to make a topping for delicious, oven-fried or broiled vegetables.
- Use oat flour as a thickener for sauces and casseroles.
- Cook whole oats or steel-cut oats in a crockpot with vegetables for an easy, no-fuss side dish.
- Add oat bran to stuffed baked potatoes.
- Cook whole oats with your favorite stuffing spices for a perfect accompaniment to any holiday meal.
- Stuff tomatoes or green peppers with cooked whole oats.

Eggplant Sticks

Ideal for a family dinner or at home at an elegant dinner party, these crusty sticks of eggplant make a unique side dish. Serve them plain or top them with your favorite marinara sauce.

Makes 6 servings

1	medium eggplant (about 1-1/4 pounds)
1/3	cup all-purpose flour
2	egg whites
1/2	cup water
3/4	cup oat bran
1/3	cup wheat germ
1-1/2	teaspoons dried oregano
1/2	teaspoon dried basil
1/4	teaspoon garlic powder
1	teaspoon paprika
	Salt and pepper to taste
4 to 5	teaspoons vegetable oil

Preheat oven to 400°.

Lightly oil a baking sheet or spray with a nonstick cooking spray.

Peel eggplant and slice lengthwise into slices 1/2- to 3/4-inch thick. Cut each slice into 1/2- to 3/4-inch strips.

Place flour in a small paper bag and put half of the eggplant strips in the bag. Close tightly and turn bag over gently several times to coat eggplant. Remove eggplant and repeat with second half.

In a shallow bowl, beat egg whites and water together with a fork.

In another shallow bowl, combine oat bran, wheat germ, and spices.

Dip floured eggplant sticks first in egg white mixture and then in oat bran, coating sticks on all sides. Place on prepared baking sheet. Drizzle sticks very lightly with oil, using about 1/8 teaspoon of oil for every 2 sticks.

Bake 25 minutes, turning sticks over halfway through the cooking time.

Serve hot.

Per serving:

148	Calories
7 g	Protein
5 g	Fat
20 g	Carbohydrate
21 mg	Sodium
0 mg	Cholesterol
4 g	Fiber

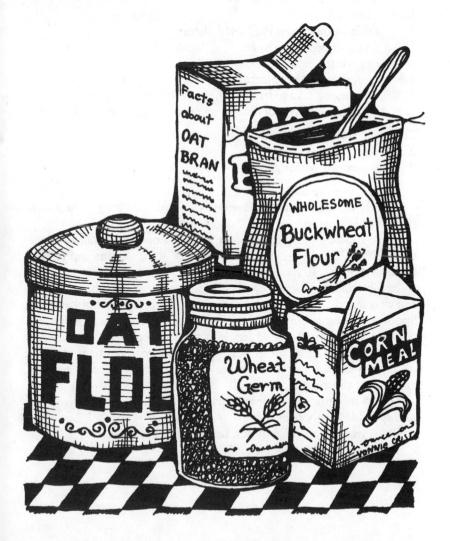

Sensational Spinach

This sensational casserole has the light, airy texture of a soufflé, combined with the wonderful flavor of spinach and onions.

Makes 6 servings

2   tablespoons olive oil
1/2   cup finely chopped onions
2   cloves garlic, minced
1-1/2   cups low-fat cottage cheese
1/3   cup oat bran
1   tablespoon grated Parmesan cheese
        Salt and pepper to taste
3   egg whites
1/4   teaspoon cream of tartar
1   10-ounce package frozen, chopped spinach, thawed and
            drained well (squeeze out as much water as possible)

Topping:
2   teaspoons oat bran
2   teaspoons wheat germ

Preheat oven to 350°.

Lightly oil a shallow 1-1/2-quart casserole or spray with a non-stick cooking spray.

Heat 1 tablespoon of the oil in a small nonstick skillet over medium heat. Add onions and garlic. Cook until onions are brown, about 5 minutes. Remove from heat.

In a blender container, combine cottage cheese, oat bran, Parmesan cheese, salt, pepper, and 1 of the egg whites. Blend until smooth. Spoon into a large bowl. Add onion mixture and spinach. Mix well.

Place remaining 2 egg whites in a small, deep bowl. Beat on low speed of an electric mixer until frothy. Add cream of tartar and beat on high speed until egg whites are stiff. Fold into spinach mixture, gently, but thoroughly.

Spoon mixture into prepared pan. Combine topping ingredients and sprinkle evenly over top.

Bake, uncovered, 35 minutes, until lightly browned.

Let stand 5 minutes before serving.

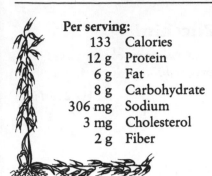

Per serving:

133	Calories
12 g	Protein
6 g	Fat
8 g	Carbohydrate
306 mg	Sodium
3 mg	Cholesterol
2 g	Fiber

Broiled Zucchini

*The combination of oat bran and Parmesan cheese makes
a delectable topping for this easy dish.*

Makes 2 servings

1	large zucchini (about 12 ounces)
2	teaspoons olive oil
2	tablespoons oat bran
2	teaspoons grated Parmesan cheese
1/8	teaspoon pepper

Lightly oil a baking sheet or spray with a nonstick cooking spray.

Slice zucchini lengthwise into 1/4-inch thick slices. Brush top side of each slice with oil.

Combine oat bran, Parmesan cheese, and pepper and sprinkle evenly over zucchini.

Place slices on prepared baking sheet.

Broil 5 to 10 minutes, until lightly browned.

Per serving:

92	Calories
4 g	Protein
6 g	Fat
8 g	Carbohydrate
36 mg	Sodium
1 mg	Cholesterol
2 g	Fiber

"Fried" Tomatoes

Use very firm, almost ripe tomatoes for this delicious side dish that goes with any entrée. Green tomatoes will also work, but they usually do not have the "tomato-ey" flavor of the more ripe ones.

Makes 4 servings

1	pound very firm tomatoes (about 3 medium tomatoes), sliced 1/2-inch thick
1	egg white
1/4	cup water
1/4	cup oat bran
1/4	cup yellow cornmeal
1/8	teaspoon garlic powder
	Salt and pepper to taste
1/4	cup all-purpose flour
4	teaspoons vegetable oil

In a small bowl, combine egg white and water. Beat with a fork or wire whisk until blended.

In another small bowl, combine oat bran, cornmeal, garlic powder, salt, and pepper. Mix well.

Place flour in a third small bowl.

One at a time, dip each tomato slice in the flour, coating each side. Then dip in the egg white mixture and finally in the oat bran mixture, again coating each side.

Preheat a large nonstick skillet or griddle over medium-high heat. Add 2 teaspoons of the oil and tilt pan back and forth to coat evenly. Cook the tomatoes until lightly browned on both sides, turning carefully and adding the rest of the oil as needed.

Serve hot.

Per serving:

147	Calories
4 g	Protein
5 g	Fat
21 g	Carbohydrate
22 mg	Sodium
0 mg	Cholesterol
3 g	Fiber

Italian Tomato Casserole

One of our quickest and easiest favorites, this side dish
casserole tastes great by itself and is also delicious
spooned over a baked potato.

Makes 4 servings

1	1-pound can salt-free (or regular) tomatoes, chopped, undrained
1/4	cup oat bran
1/2	cup water
1	tablespoon minced onion flakes
1	teaspoon dried oregano
1/2	teaspoon dried basil
1/8	teaspoon garlic powder
	Salt and pepper to taste

Preheat oven to 350°.

Lightly oil a 1-quart baking dish or spray with a nonstick cooking spray.

Combine all ingredients in a bowl and mix well. Place in prepared dish.

Bake, uncovered, 45 minutes.

Serve hot.

Per serving:

48	Calories
2 g	Protein
1 g	Fat
9 g	Carbohydrate
15 mg	Sodium
0 mg	Cholesterol
2 g	Fiber

Granola-Stuffed Acorn Squash

"Pretty as a picture," this elegant side dish will add a
festive touch to any meal.

Makes 4 servings

2	medium acorn squash, split and seeded
1/2	cup granola (page 16)*
1	large, sweet apple, unpeeled, coarsely shredded (1 cup)
1	teaspoon grated fresh orange rind
2	teaspoons honey *or* maple syrup
2	teaspoons vegetable oil

Preheat oven to 350°.

Lightly oil a shallow baking pan or spray with a nonstick cooking spray.

Place squash in prepared pan. (Slice a thin piece off the bottom of each squash to keep it from tipping over in the pan.)

Combine granola, apple, and orange rind. Divide mixture evenly and pile into the squash cavities.

Drizzle the tops with honey and oil.

Bake 30 minutes.

Fold a piece of foil into a tent and lay it loosely over the squash to keep it from getting too brown.

Bake 30 minutes more.

*Commercial granolas will also work, but read the labels carefully because many of them are loaded with fat.

Per serving:

180	Calories
3 g	Protein
5 g	Fat
35 g	Carbohydrate
7 mg	Sodium
0 mg	Cholesterol
8 g	Fiber

Broccoli Bonanza

This wonderful casserole of broccoli and Cheddar cheese on an oat crust is a family-pleaser as well as a great party dish.

Makes 8 servings

1   1-pound package frozen, chopped broccoli

Crust:
1/4   cup oat bran
1/4   cup whole wheat flour
1/4   cup yellow cornmeal
1   teaspoon baking powder
1/8   teaspoon pepper
1   teaspoon dried oregano
1/8   teaspoon garlic powder
2   egg whites
1/2   cup skim milk

Topping:
3/4   cup shredded low-fat Cheddar cheese
1/2   cup skim milk
2   egg whites
1   tablespoon minced onion flakes
1/8   teaspoon garlic powder
         Salt to taste

Preheat oven to 350°.

Lightly oil an 8-inch square baking pan or spray with a nonstick cooking spray.

Cook broccoli according to package directions. Drain well.

To prepare crust:

In a large bowl, combine dry crust ingredients and spices. Mix well. In a small bowl, combine egg whites and milk. Beat with a fork or wire whisk until blended. Add to dry mixture, mixing until all ingredients are moistened. Spread mixture evenly in prepared pan.

Spoon broccoli evenly over crust. With the back of a spoon, press broccoli down firmly into crust.

To prepare topping:

Sprinkle cheddar cheese evenly over broccoli.

In a blender container, combine remaining ingredients. Blend until smooth. Pour over broccoli and cheese. Press down gently so that broccoli is moistened.

Bake, uncovered, 30 minutes, until set.

Cut into squares; serve hot.

Per serving:

111	Calories
8 g	Protein
2 g	Fat
17 g	Carbohydrate
141 mg	Sodium
4 mg	Cholesterol
2 g	Fiber

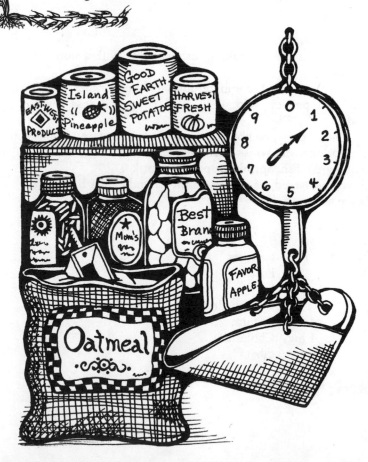

Corn Pudding

The addition of oat flour to this custardy dish gives it a new, velvety texture. Besides a side dish, it's great for brunch.

Makes 6 servings

1/3	cup oat flour
1/2	teaspoon baking powder
	Salt and pepper to taste
2	teaspoons dried chives
1	teaspoon dried parsley flakes
1	10-ounce package frozen corn, thawed
3	egg whites
1	cup skim milk
1	tablespoon vegetable oil
1	tablespoon honey
	Paprika

Preheat oven to 350°.

Lightly oil a 1-quart baking dish or spray with a nonstick cooking spray.

In a medium bowl, combine flour, baking powder, salt, pepper, chives, and parsley. Mix well. Add corn and toss until evenly coated.

In a small bowl, combine egg whites, milk, oil, and honey. Beat with a fork or wire whisk until blended. Stir into dry mixture. Pour into prepared dish. Sprinkle top with paprika.

Bake, uncovered, 35 minutes until set and lightly browned.

Serve hot.

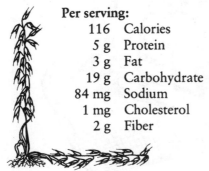

Per serving:

116	Calories
5 g	Protein
3 g	Fat
19 g	Carbohydrate
84 mg	Sodium
1 mg	Cholesterol
2 g	Fiber

Potato–Oat Pancakes

This brand new version of an old favorite has all the flavor of the original, with added nutrition. These pancakes make a versatile side dish that goes with almost any entrée. Or, try them topped with applesauce for a special brunch dish.

Makes 18 three-inch pancakes

2	large potatoes (about 1-1/2 pounds total), unpeeled, cut into cubes
1	small onion, coarsely chopped
1	teaspoon lemon juice
1/2	teaspoon baking powder
1/2	teaspoon salt
1/8	teaspoon pepper
3/4	cup rolled oats

In a blender container, combine potatoes, onion, and lemon juice. Blend until smooth. Pour mixture into a large bowl.

Add baking powder, salt, pepper, and oats, mixing well. Let mixture stand 15 minutes.

Preheat a nonstick skillet or griddle over medium heat. Oil it lightly or spray with a nonstick cooking spray. Drop potato mixture onto griddle, using 2 tablespoonfuls for each pancake. Cook pancakes until brown on both sides, turning carefully.

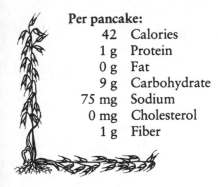

Per pancake:

42	Calories
1 g	Protein
0 g	Fat
9 g	Carbohydrate
75 mg	Sodium
0 mg	Cholesterol
1 g	Fiber

Cheesy Stuffed Potatoes

There are many versions of this popular twice-baked potato dish. This one combines two kinds of cheese with oat bran for a delicious difference. It serves 4 as a side dish or 2 as a filling entrée.

Makes 4 servings

2	medium potatoes (8 ounces each), baked
1/4	cup oat bran
1/2	cup low-fat cottage cheese
1/4	cup shredded low-fat Cheddar cheese
2	teaspoons Dijon mustard
1/4	cup plus 2 tablespoons skim milk
1/8	teaspoon pepper
	Salt to taste
	Paprika

Preheat oven to 375°.

Lightly oil a shallow baking pan or spray with a nonstick cooking spray.

Cut potatoes in half lengthwise. Carefully scoop out pulp with a spoon, leaving a 1/4-inch shell.

Place potato pulp in a large bowl. Add remaining ingredients, *except* paprika. Mash with a fork or potato masher until mixture is well blended.

Spoon mixture into potato shells, smoothing the tops.

Spinkle with paprika.

Bake 30 minutes, uncovered.

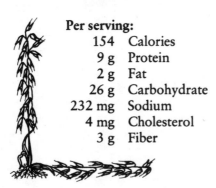

Per serving:
154	Calories
9 g	Protein
2 g	Fat
26 g	Carbohydrate
232 mg	Sodium
4 mg	Cholesterol
3 g	Fiber

Potato Kugel

Hearty, moist, and very filling, this old-time potato
pudding will complement any meal.

Makes 6 servings

2	large potatoes (about 1-1/2 pounds total), unpeeled, cut into cubes
1	small onion, coarsely chopped
1	teaspoon lemon juice
2	tablespoons vegetable oil
1	teaspoon baking powder
3/4	teaspoon salt
1/8	teaspoon pepper
1/4	cup oat bran

Preheat oven to 350°.

Lightly oil a 1-quart baking dish or spray with a nonstick cooking spray.

In a blender container, combine potatoes, onion, lemon juice, and oil. Blend until smooth.

Add remaining ingredients. Blend until combined. Spoon mixture into prepared pan.

Bake, uncovered, 1 hour.

Serve hot.

Per serving:

141	Calories
3 g	Protein
5 g	Fat
22 g	Carbohydrate
354 mg	Sodium
0 mg	Cholesterol
3 g	Fiber

Pepper and Onion Squares

Sautéed onions and green peppers atop a moist bread-like crust make this side dish one to remember.

Makes 8 servings

Topping:
2   tablespoons olive oil
1-1/2   cups chopped onions
1-1/2   cups chopped green pepper
3   cloves garlic, minced

Crust:
1/3   cup oat bran
1/3   cup rolled oats
1/3   cup whole wheat flour
1   tablespoon grated Parmesan cheese
1   teaspoon baking powder
2   egg whites
1/2   cup skim milk

Preheat oven to 350°.
Lightly oil an 8-inch square baking pan or spray with a nonstick cooking spray.

To prepare topping:
Heat oil in a large nonstick skillet over medium heat. Add onions, green pepper, and garlic. Cook until tender, about 10 minutes. Remove from heat.

To prepare crust:
In a medium bowl, combine oat bran, oats, flour, Parmesan cheese, and baking powder. Mix well.
In a small bowl, combine egg whites and milk. Beat with a fork or wire whisk until blended. Add to oat mixture, mixing until all ingredients are moistened. Spread mixture evenly in the bottom of prepared pan.
Spread onion mixture evenly over batter. Press down into batter with the back of a spoon.
Bake 25 minutes, uncovered.
Cut into squares to serve. Serve hot.

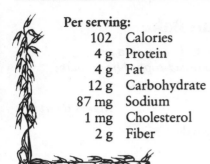

Per serving:

102	Calories
4 g	Protein
4 g	Fat
12 g	Carbohydrate
87 mg	Sodium
1 mg	Cholesterol
2 g	Fiber

Easy Bean Bake

*Now you can turn ordinary baked beans into an
extraordinary side dish. These bread-topped beans make
a 1-2-3 addition to any cookout or family dinner.*

Makes 6 servings

1	1-pound can vegetarian-style baked beans
1/3	cup oat bran
1/3	cup yellow cornmeal
1/3	cup whole wheat flour
1/4	cup nonfat dry milk
1	teaspoon baking powder
1/2	teaspoon baking soda
1	cup water
2	tablespoons vegetable oil

Preheat oven to 350°.

Lightly oil a 6 x 10-inch baking pan or spray with a nonstick cooking spray.

Spread beans in the bottom of prepared pan.

In a medium bowl, combine oat bran, cornmeal, flour, dry milk, baking powder, and baking soda. Mix well. Add water and oil. Beat with a fork or wire whisk until all ingredients are moistened (batter may be lumpy). Pour over beans.

Bake 30 minutes, until topping is set and lightly browned.

Serve hot.

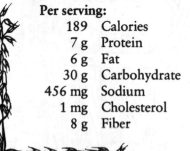

Per serving:

189	Calories
7 g	Protein
6 g	Fat
30 g	Carbohydrate
456 mg	Sodium
1 mg	Cholesterol
8 g	Fiber

Dusty Cauliflower

This is truly cauliflower at its best! For a spectacular variation, try "Dusty Mushrooms." Simply replace the cauliflower with 4 cups of fresh mushrooms, cut into halves or quarters. Either way, it's great!

Makes 6 servings

4	cups cauliflower, cut into small flowerets
2	tablespoons vegetable oil
3	tablespoons oat bran
3	tablespoons dry bread crumbs
1	tablespoon plus 1 teaspoon grated Parmesan cheese
1/8	teaspoon pepper
	Dash garlic powder

Preheat oven to 400°.

Lightly oil a 10 x 15-inch baking pan or spray with a nonstick cooking spray.

Place cauliflower in a large bowl. Drizzle with oil and toss until cauliflower is evenly coated.

Combine remaining ingredients and sprinkle over cauliflower. Toss until coated.

Spread cauliflower in prepared pan and sprinkle with any remaining crumbs.

Bake 18 to 20 minutes, until lightly browned.

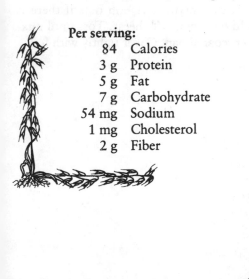

Per serving:

84	Calories
3 g	Protein
5 g	Fat
7 g	Carbohydrate
54 mg	Sodium
1 mg	Cholesterol
2 g	Fiber

Cauliflower and Oats

This flavorful dish combines cauliflower and oats with the delightful tastes of garlic and cheese. You'll love the results.

Makes 6 servings

2/3	cup whole oats (groats)
2	cups water
2	tablespoons olive oil
1	cup chopped onions
2	cloves garlic, minced
3	cups cauliflower, cut into 1-inch flowerets
1/2	cup low-fat cottage cheese
1/2	cup shredded low-fat Cheddar cheese

Combine water and oats in a large saucepan. Bring to a boil over medium heat. Reduce heat to low, cover, and cook 40 to 45 minutes, stirring occasionally.

While oats are cooking, prepare cauliflower: Heat oil in a large nonstick skillet over medium heat. Add onions and garlic. Cook 5 minutes, stirring frequently. Add cauliflower and cook 5 minutes more, continuing to stir frequently. Remove from heat.

Preheat oven to 350°.

Lightly oil an 8-inch square baking pan or spray with a nonstick cooking spray.

Add cooked oats to cauliflower mixture. (Drain oats if there is still water left in the pot.) Add both types of cheese. Toss until mixture is combined. Spoon into prepared pan. Cover tightly with foil.

Bake 30 minutes.

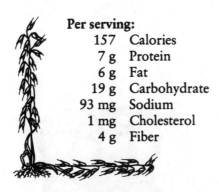

Per serving:

157	Calories
7 g	Protein
6 g	Fat
19 g	Carbohydrate
93 mg	Sodium
1 mg	Cholesterol
4 g	Fiber

Toasted Oat and Mushroom Bake

This is one of our very favorite side dishes. Toasting the oats gives them a wonderful flavor.

Makes 8 servings

3	tablespoons vegetable oil
1	cup steel-cut oats
3/4	cup rolled oats
3-3/4	cups hot water
1	cup chopped onions
1	clove garlic, minced
3/4	pound mushrooms, sliced
2	tablespoons reduced-sodium (or regular) soy sauce
1	teaspoon dried basil
	Pepper to taste

Heat 2 tablespoons of the oil in a large saucepan over medium heat. Add both types of oats. Cook, stirring constantly, until oats are lightly toasted, about 8 minutes. Add hot water, reduce heat to low, cover, and simmer 20 minutes.

While oats are cooking, heat remaining tablespoon of oil in a large nonstick skillet over medium heat. Add onions and garlic. Cook 10 minutes, stirring frequently, until onions are tender and start to brown. Add mushrooms. Cook 10 minutes more, stirring frequently. Remove from heat.

Preheat oven to 375°.

Lightly oil an 8-inch square baking pan or spray with a nonstick cooking spray.

When oats are finished cooking, stir in soy sauce, basil, and pepper. Then add mushroom mixture. Mix well. Spoon into prepared pan. Cover and bake 20 minutes.

Per serving:

180	Calories
6 g	Protein
7 g	Fat
24 g	Carbohydrate
153 mg	Sodium
0 mg	Cholesterol
4 g	Fiber

Onions, Mushrooms and Oats

The flavor of this delicately spiced side dish is reminiscent of a delicious Thanksgiving stuffing.

Makes 6 servings

2	tablespoons vegetable oil
1	cup chopped onions
2	cups sliced mushrooms
1	clove garlic, minced
3	cups water
1	cup whole oats (groats)
1/4	teaspoon dried thyme
1/4	teaspoon ground sage
1/4	teaspoon poultry seasoning
	Salt and pepper to taste

Heat oil in a large saucepan over medium heat. Add onions, mushrooms, and garlic. Cook 10 minutes, until onions are tender and begin to brown. Stir frequently and add small amounts of water, if necessary, to prevent sticking.

Add remaining ingredients and bring to a boil. Cover, reduce heat to low, and simmer 45 to 50 minutes, until oats are tender and most of the liquid has been absorbed. Stir occasionally while cooking.

Remove from heat and let stand, covered, 5 minutes before serving.

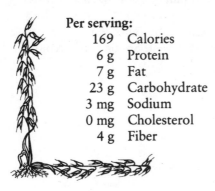

Per serving:

169	Calories
6 g	Protein
7 g	Fat
23 g	Carbohydrate
3 mg	Sodium
0 mg	Cholesterol
4 g	Fiber

Sherried Orange Oats

Slightly sweet, with the pleasant taste of sherry, this dish makes a perfect accompaniment to any of your favorite entrées.

Makes 6 servings

1	cup whole oats (groats)
1/2	teaspoon dried thyme
1	packet instant, low-sodium, chicken-flavored broth mix (or vegetable broth mix)
1	tablespoon minced onion flakes
2	cups water
3/4	cup orange juice (unsweetened)
1/4	cup dry sherry
	Salt and pepper to taste

Combine all ingredients in a medium saucepan. Bring to a boil over medium heat. Reduce heat to low, cover, and simmer 45 to 50 minutes, until oats are tender and most of the liquid has been absorbed. Remove from heat and let stand, covered, 5 minutes before serving.

Per serving:
- 136 Calories
- 5 g Protein
- 2 g Fat
- 25 g Carbohydrate
- 3 mg Sodium
- 0 mg Cholesterol
- 3 g Fiber

Curried Oats

*For an extra touch, you may want to add raisins or
chopped peanuts to this Indian favorite. If so, add them
during the last 15 minutes of cooking time.*

Makes 6 servings

1   cup whole oats (groats)
3   cups water
3/4   teaspoon ground turmeric
3/4   teaspoon curry powder
1/8   teaspoon ground cinnamon
2   packets instant low-sodium chicken-flavored broth mix (or
       vegetable broth mix)

Combine all ingredients in a large saucepan. Bring to a boil over medium heat. Reduce heat to low, cover, and simmer 45 to 50 minutes, until oats are tender and liquid is absorbed. Stir occasionally while cooking. (Stir more frequently near end of cooking time to keep oats from sticking.)
Serve hot.

Per serving:
   119 Calories
    5 g Protein
    2 g Fat
   21 g Carbohydrate
   3 mg Sodium
   0 mg Cholesterol
    3 g Fiber

Spanish Oats

Usually made with rice, this tasty and colorful side dish goes especially well with baked chicken or fish. And, it couldn't be easier!

Makes 6 servings

1	15-ounce can stewed tomatoes
1	teaspoon chili powder
2/3	cup whole oats (groats)
2	cups water

In a large saucepan, combine all ingredients. Bring to a boil over medium heat. Reduce heat to low, cover, and simmer 1 hour until oats are tender and most of liquid is absorbed. Stir occasionally while cooking.

Remove from heat and let stand, covered, 5 minutes before serving.

Per serving:

95	Calories
4 g	Protein
1 g	Fat
18 g	Carbohydrate
185 mg	Sodium
0 mg	Cholesterol
2 g	Fiber

Corny Casserole

This tasty side dish can easily be made into an entrée. Just add cooked chicken chunks, shrimp, tuna, or a can of kidney beans.

Makes 6 servings

1	tablespoon olive oil
1	cup chopped onions
1	cup chopped green pepper
2	cups sliced mushrooms
1	8-ounce can salt-free (or regular) tomato sauce
2	cups cooked whole oats (groats) (see cooking directions on page 6)
1	cup canned cream-style corn
1	teaspoon dried basil
	Salt and pepper to taste

Preheat oven to 350°.

Lightly oil a 1-3/4 quart casserole or spray with a nonstick cooking spray.

Heat oil in a large nonstick skillet over medium heat. Add onions and green pepper. Cook 5 minutes, until tender. Add a small amount of water, if necessary, to prevent drying.

Add mushrooms. Cook 5 minutes, stirring frequently.

Add remaining ingredients, mixing well. Place mixture in prepared casserole.

Cover and bake 20 minutes.

Uncover and bake 20 minutes more.

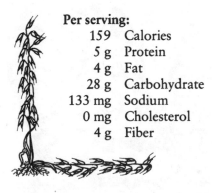

Per serving:

159	Calories
5 g	Protein
4 g	Fat
28 g	Carbohydrate
133 mg	Sodium
0 mg	Cholesterol
4 g	Fiber

Crockpot Oats and Beans

This hearty side dish can also be used to serve 4 to 6 as a delicious meatless entrée.

Makes 8 servings

1	cup whole oats (groats)
1	cup chopped onions
1/2	cup sliced carrots, 1/2-inch thick
1	1-pound can kidney beans, rinsed and drained
1/4	teaspoon garlic powder
1/2	teaspoon dried thyme
1	bay leaf
1	8-ounce can salt-free (or regular) tomato sauce
2-1/2	cups water
	Salt and pepper to taste

In a large crockpot, combine all ingredients. Mix well. Cover and cook 2 hours on high setting.

Reduce heat to low, stir mixture, cover, and cook 4-1/2 to 5 hours.

Remove and discard bay leaf before serving.

Per serving:

151	Calories
7 g	Protein
2 g	Fat
28 g	Carbohydrate
207 mg	Sodium
0 mg	Cholesterol
7 g	Fiber

Oat-Stuffed Tomatoes

This unique combination of tomatoes and oats makes a colorful, as well as tasty, side dish. Try the leftovers cold as a quick, nutritious lunchtime salad.

Makes 4 servings

4	large tomatoes
1/2	cup cooked whole oats (groats) (see cooking directions on page 6)
1/8	teaspoon garlic powder
1/2	teaspoon dried oregano
1/2	teaspoon dried basil
1/8	teaspoon pepper
1/4	teaspoon sugar
1/4	cup finely chopped green onion (green part only)
2	ounces shredded part-skim Mozzarella cheese
	Salt to taste

Preheat oven to 350°.

Lighty oil a shallow baking pan or spray with a nonstick cooking spray.

Cut a thin slice off the top of each tomato. With a knife or spoon, carefully scoop out the pulp. Chop pulp and place in a large bowl.

Add remaining ingredients and mix well. Spoon into tomato shells. Place in prepared pan. (Place tomatoes close together to keep them from tipping over, or slice a *very* thin slice off the bottom of each one, being careful not to cut all the way through.)

Bake, uncovered, 30 minutes.

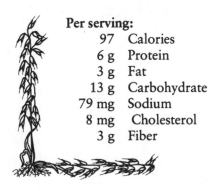

Per serving:

97	Calories
6 g	Protein
3 g	Fat
13 g	Carbohydrate
79 mg	Sodium
8 mg	Cholesterol
3 g	Fiber

Golden Carrot Oats

*These oats are cooked with onions and carrots and are
reminiscent of Mom's homemade chicken soup. It's a
wonderful side dish to serve with roast chicken or turkey.*

Makes 6 servings

2	tablespoons olive oil
1	cup finely chopped onions
3	cups water
2	packets instant low-sodium chicken-flavored broth mix (or vegetable broth mix)
1	cup whole oats (groats)
1	cup finely shredded carrots
	Salt and pepper to taste

Heat oil in a large saucepan over medium heat. Add onions.
Cook 10 minutes, until lightly browned. Stir frequently to avoid
sticking.

Add remaining ingredients and bring to a boil. Cover, reduce
heat to low, and simmer 45 to 50 minutes, until oats are tender and
most of the liquid has been absorbed.

Let stand, covered, 5 minutes before serving.

Per serving:

173	Calories
5 g	Protein
6 g	Fat
24 g	Carbohydrate
10 mg	Sodium
0 mg	Cholesterol
4 g	Fiber

Mixed Grains

You can add any spices you like to this wonderfully textured combination of grains. Or, top them with your favorite pasta or Oriental sauce. Try the cold leftovers with skim milk and raisins for a delicious change-of-pace breakfast.

Makes 4 servings

2   cups water
2/3   cup mixed whole oats (groats), barley, and brown rice (equal parts of each)

Combine grains and water in a large saucepan over medium heat. Bring to a boil. Reduce heat to low, cover, and simmer 40 to 45 minutes, until grains are tender and most of the water is absorbed. (Because stove-top temperatures and types of saucepans vary, check grains periodically and add more water, if necessary.)
Drain and serve.

Per serving:
   112   Calories
    4 g   Protein
    1 g   Fat
   22 g   Carbohydrate
   2 mg   Sodium
   0 mg   Cholesterol
    3 g   Fiber

Herbed Oats and Wild Rice

This side dish is truly a gourmet's delight—and it's so easy!

Makes 6 servings

1/2	cup whole oats (groats)
1/2	cup wild rice
3	cups water
2	teaspoons sesame oil
1/2	teaspoon dried rosemary, crumbled (crumble before measuring)
1/4	teaspoon dried basil
1/2	teaspoon dried oregano
1/4	teaspoon dried thyme
1/2	teaspoon dill weed
2	teaspoons dried chives

Combine all ingredients in a large saucepan. Bring to a boil over medium heat. Reduce heat to low, cover, and cook 45 to 50 minutes, until oats are tender and most of the liquid has been absorbed. Stir occasionally while cooking.

Let stand, covered, 5 minutes before serving.

Per serving:

118	Calories
4 g	Protein
3 g	Fat
20 g	Carbohydrate
2 mg	Sodium
0 mg	Cholesterol
2 g	Fiber

Breads

Adding the whole-grain goodness of oats to breads is an easy task. The mellow, "oaty" flavor imparts a naturally delicious taste and texture that can't be beat. In fact, oats seem to actually sweeten the dough. This section contains two types of breads—quick breads and yeast breads. In all of them, I have added other high-fiber ingredients (both soluble and insoluble fiber) for added nutrition and flavor.

I found that in most bread recipes I was able to substitute about one-third of the flour with oat bran or rolled oats. Because oats contain no gluten, they are generally used in combination with wheat flour, which is rich in gluten, so that they will rise.

Most of the breads in this section are sweetened with honey, molasses, or pure maple syrup. I found that using a sweetening agent in a liquid form enabled me to greatly reduce the amount of oil in a recipe and still retain a pleasant, moist texture while greatly reducing the fat content.

To limit the amounts of saturated fat and cholesterol, these recipes use only skim milk and low-fat dairy products, and egg whites in place of whole eggs.

When baking quick breads, generally the dry ingredients are combined and the liquid ingredients are whisked together and added to the dry. When doing this, stir just until all ingredients are moistened. Avoid overmixing, which can sometimes toughen the dough.

Remember that oven temperatures vary, and the cooking times are suggested times. Most quick breads can be tested with a toothpick for doneness. (A toothpick inserted in the center of the bread will come out clean when the bread is done.)

Home-baked breads are at their best when eaten the same day and are easiest to slice after they have cooled completely. Remember that these breads, unlike most commercially-baked goods, contain no preservatives and therefore have a shorter shelf life. I found that on the second day it is best to store these breads in the refrigerator (or freezer) and either toast them or reheat them in a microwave for a few seconds before serving.

The following are some ideas to help you add the sweetness and fiber of oats to your own bread recipes:

- Replace one-fourth to one-third of the flour with oat bran.
- Sprinkle rolled oats over the top of breads before baking.

- Combine rolled oats with sugar and cinnamon for a delicious, sweet topping.
- Mix oat bran with wheat germ and cinnamon for another topping variation.
- Replace one-third of the cornmeal with oat bran in your favorite cornbread recipe.

  Be sure to read the suggestions for baking yeast breads on page 153.

Fruity Oat Bran Bread

In place of a pear, this bread is delicious with a peach.

Makes 12 servings

3/4	cup whole wheat flour
1/2	cup oat bran
1/3	cup wheat bran
1	teaspoon baking soda
1/2	teaspoon baking powder
1	teaspoon ground cinnamon
1/4	teaspoon ground nutmeg
2	egg whites
1	tablespoon vegetable oil
1/4	cup honey
1/3	cup apple juice
1/2	cup water
1	teaspoon vanilla extract
1/2	teaspoon orange extract
1/4	cup raisins
1	large, sweet pear, unpeeled, finely chopped (about 1 cup)

Preheat oven to 350°.

Lightly oil a 4 x 8-inch loaf pan or spray with a nonstick cooking spray.

In a large bowl, combine dry ingredients, mixing well.

In another bowl, combine remaining ingredients, *except* raisins and chopped pear. Beat with a fork or wire whisk until blended. Add to dry ingredients, along with raisins and pear. Stir until all ingredients are moistened. Place mixture in prepared pan.

Bake 50 minutes, until a toothpick inserted in the center of the bread comes out clean.

Cool in pan 5 minutes, then transfer to a rack to finish cooling.

Per serving:

101	Calories
3 g	Protein
2 g	Fat
20 g	Carbohydrate
96 mg	Sodium
0 mg	Cholesterol
3 g	Fiber

Pineapple Pecan Loaf

The combination of crushed pineapple and rolled oats
gives this fruity bread a wonderful texture.

Makes 12 servings

1/2	cup whole wheat flour
1/2	cup all-purpose flour
1	cup rolled oats
1	teaspoon baking powder
1	teaspoon baking soda
1/4	cup chopped pecans
1/4	cup firmly packed brown sugar
3	tablespoons vegetable oil
1	teaspoon vanilla extract
2	egg whites
1/3	cup plus 1 tablespoon orange juice (unsweetened)
1/2	teaspoon orange extract
1	cup canned crushed pineapple (unsweetened), undrained

Preheat oven to 350°.

Lightly oil a 4 x 8-inch loaf pan or spray with a nonstick cooking spray.

In a large bowl, combine both types of flour, oats, baking powder, baking soda, and pecans. Mix well.

In another bowl, combine remaining ingredients, *except* pineapple. Beat with a fork or wire whisk until blended. Stir in pineapple. Add to dry mixture, stirring until all ingredients are moistened.

Place in prepared pan.

Bake 40 to 45 minutes, until a toothpick inserted in the center of the bread comes out clean.

Cool in pan 5 minutes, then transfer to a rack to finish cooling.

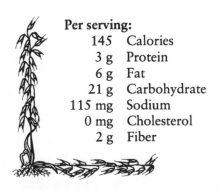

Per serving:

145	Calories
3 g	Protein
6 g	Fat
21 g	Carbohydrate
115 mg	Sodium
0 mg	Cholesterol
2 g	Fiber

Applesauce Cornbread

This moist cornbread is slightly sweet and makes a perfect accompaniment to any meal.

Makes 12 servings

3/4	cup yellow cornmeal
1/2	cup oat bran
1/4	cup all-purpose flour
1/4	cup whole wheat flour
2	teaspoons baking powder
1-1/4	teaspoons ground cinnamon
1	cup applesauce (unsweetened)
1/2	cup skim milk
2	egg whites
1	teaspoon vanilla extract
1	tablespoon vegetable oil
3	tablespoons honey

Preheat oven to 375°

Lightly oil a 6 x 10-inch baking pan or spray with a nonstick cooking spray.

In a large bowl, combine dry ingredients. Mix well.

In another bowl, combine remaining ingredients. Beat with a fork or wire whisk until blended. Add to dry mixture, mixing just until all ingredients are moistened.

Place mixture in prepared pan.

Bake 25 minutes, until firm.

Cool in pan on a rack.

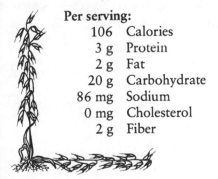

Per serving:

106	Calories
3 g	Protein
2 g	Fat
20 g	Carbohydrate
86 mg	Sodium
0 mg	Cholesterol
2 g	Fiber

Carrot Spice Bread

Applesauce and carrots, along with a delicious blend of spices, make this bread a hit—and healthy, too!

Makes 14 servings

1-1/2 cups whole wheat flour
1/2   cup all-purpose flour
3/4   cup oat bran
1/2   teaspoon baking soda
1   teaspoon baking powder
1-1/2 teaspoons ground cinnamon
1/4   teaspoon ground nutmeg
1/8   teaspoon ground allspice
1/8   teaspoon ground cloves
2   egg whites
1   cup applesauce (unsweetened)
1/3   cup water
3   tablespoons vegetable oil
1/3   cup honey
1   teaspoon vanilla extract
1   cup finely shredded carrots
1/3   cup raisins

Preheat oven to 350°.

Lightly oil a 5 x 9-inch loaf pan or spray with a nonstick cooking spray.

In a large bowl, combine both types of flour, oat bran, baking soda, baking powder, and spices. Mix well.

In another bowl, combine remaining ingredients, *except* carrots and raisins. Beat with a fork or wire whisk until blended. Add to dry mixture, along with carrots and raisins. Mix until all ingredients are moistened.

Place in prepared pan.

Bake 45 to 50 minutes, until a toothpick inserted in the center of the bread comes out clean.

Cool in pan 5 minutes, then transfer to a rack to finish cooling.

Per serving:

152	Calories
4 g	Protein
4 g	Fat
28 g	Carbohydrate
71 mg	Sodium
0 mg	Cholesterol
3 g	Fiber

Apple Double Oat Bread

A combination of apples, oats, and oat bran, with lots of spices, makes this a high-fiber bread you'll really love.

Makes 12 servings

1/2	cup whole wheat flour
1/2	cup all-purpose flour
1/4	cup *each* oat bran and rolled oats
1	teaspoon *each* baking soda and baking powder
1	teaspoon ground cinnamon
1/2	teaspoon ground nutmeg
3	tablespoons slivered almonds
2	tablespoons vegetable oil
1/4	cup honey
1/2	cup apple juice
1	teaspoon vanilla extract
2	egg whites
1	large, sweet apple, unpeeled, coarsely shredded (about 1 cup)

Preheat oven to 350°.

Lightly oil a 4 x 8-inch loaf pan or spray with a nonstick cooking spray.

In a large bowl, combine flour, oat bran, oats, baking soda, baking powder, spices, and almonds. Mix well.

In another bowl, combine remaining ingredients, *except* apple. Beat with a fork or wire whisk until blended. Add to dry ingredients, along with apples. Mix until all ingredients are moistened.

Place mixture in prepared pan.

Bake 40 to 45 minutes, until a toothpick inserted in the center of the bread comes out clean.

Cool in pan 5 minutes, then transfer to a rack to finish cooling.

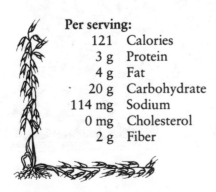

Per serving:

121	Calories
3 g	Protein
4 g	Fat
20 g	Carbohydrate
114 mg	Sodium
0 mg	Cholesterol
2 g	Fiber

Lemon Poppy Seed Bread

*You'll love the cool taste of lemon and the subtle crunch
of poppy seeds in this delectable bread.*

Makes 12 servings

3/4	cup whole wheat flour
1/2	cup all-purpose flour
1/2	cup oat bran
2	teaspoons baking powder
1	teaspoon poppy seeds
2	egg whites
2	tablespoons vegetable oil
1/4	cup honey
1	cup plus 2 tablespoons skim milk
1	tablespoon grated fresh lemon peel
1	teaspoon vanilla extract
1/2	teaspoon lemon extract

Preheat oven to 350°.

Lightly oil a 4 x 8-inch loaf pan or spray with a nonstick cooking spray.

In a large bowl, combine both types of flour, oat bran, baking powder, and poppy seeds. Mix well.

In another bowl, combine remaining ingredients. Beat with a fork or wire whisk until blended. Add to dry mixture, mixing until all ingredients are moistened.

Place mixture in prepared pan.

Bake 40 minutes, until a toothpick inserted in the center of the bread comes out clean.

Cool in pan 5 minutes, then transfer to a rack to finish cooling.

Per serving:

114	Calories
4 g	Protein
3 g	Fat
19 g	Carbohydrate
92 mg	Sodium
0 mg	Cholesterol
2 g	Fiber

Zucchini Bread

Oat bran added to this spicy favorite makes it more nutritious than ever. And, it has a moist texture you'll love.

Makes 12 servings

1/2	cup whole wheat flour
1/4	cup all-purpose flour
1/2	cup oat bran
1/4	cup rolled oats
1	teaspoon baking soda
1/2	teaspoon baking powder
1	teaspoon ground cinnamon
1/2	teaspoon ground nutmeg
1/4	teaspoon ground allspice
1/8	teaspoon ground cloves
1/2	cup skim milk
2	egg whites
2	tablespoons vegetable oil
1	teaspoon vanilla extract
1/4	cup sugar
1	cup finely shredded zucchini, unpeeled (packed tight)
1/2	cup raisins

Preheat oven to 350°.

Lightly oil a 4 x 8-inch loaf pan or spray with a nonstick cooking spray.

In a large bowl, combine dry ingredients, mixing well.

In another bowl, combine milk, egg whites, oil, vanilla, and sugar. Beat with a fork or wire whisk until blended. Stir in zucchini. Add to dry mixture, along with raisins, mixing until all ingredients are moistened.

Place mixture in prepared pan.

Bake 35 to 40 minutes, until a toothpick inserted in the center of the bread comes out clean.

Cool in pan 5 minutes, then transfer to a rack to finish cooling.

Per serving:

111	Calories
3 g	Protein
3 g	Fat
19 g	Carbohydrate
102 mg	Sodium
0 mg	Cholesterol
2 g	Fiber

Grape Nutty Bread

The crunchy cereal nuggets give this bread an unusual taste and a subtle sweetness that can't be beat.

Makes 14 servings

1/2	cup whole wheat flour
1/2	cup all-purpose flour
1/2	cup oat bran
2/3	cup Grape Nuts® cereal
1	teaspoon baking powder
1	teaspoon baking soda
1-1/2	teaspoons ground cinnamon
1	cup skim milk
1	tablespoon lemon juice
1/2	cup water
2	egg whites
1/4	cup vegetable oil
1/4	cup honey
2	teaspoons vanilla extract

Preheat oven to 350°.

Lightly oil a 5 x 9-inch loaf pan or spray with a nonstick cooking spray.

In a large bowl, combine dry ingredients. Mix well.

In another bowl, add lemon juice to milk. Let stand 1 minute. Add remaining ingredients. Beat with a fork or wire whisk until blended. Add to dry mixture, stirring until all ingredients are moistened.

Place mixture in prepared pan.

Bake 45 to 50 minutes, until a toothpick inserted in the center of the bread comes out clean.

Cool in pan 5 minutes, then transfer to a rack to finish cooling.

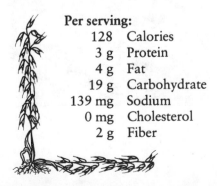

Per serving:

128	Calories
3 g	Protein
4 g	Fat
19 g	Carbohydrate
139 mg	Sodium
0 mg	Cholesterol
2 g	Fiber

Date Nut Bread

For a delicious variation, try dried apricots in place of the dates.

Makes 12 servings

3/4	cup whole wheat flour
1/2	cup *each* all-purpose flour and oat bran
2	teaspoons baking powder
1/2	teaspoon baking soda
1	teaspoon ground cinnamon
1/8	teaspoon ground allspice
1	cup skim milk
1	tablespoon lemon juice
2	egg whites
1/4	cup molasses
2	tablespoons vegetable oil
1	teaspoon vanilla extract
1/4	teaspoon lemon extract
1/2	cup chopped dried dates
1/4	cup chopped walnuts

Preheat oven to 350°.

Lightly oil a 4 x 8-inch loaf pan or spray with a nonstick cooking spray.

In a large bowl, combine dry ingredients, mixing well.

In another bowl, add lemon juice to milk. Let stand 1 minute. Add remaining ingredients, *except* dates and walnuts. Beat with a fork or wire whisk until blended. Add to dry ingredients, along with dates and nuts, stirring until all ingredients are moistened.

Place mixture in prepared pan.

Bake 35 to 40 minutes, until a toothpick inserted in the center of the bread comes out clean.

Cool in pan 5 minutes, then transfer to a rack to finish cooling.

Per serving:

144	Calories
4 g	Protein
4 g	Fat
23 g	Carbohydrate
126 mg	Sodium
0 mg	Cholesterol
2 g	Fiber

Golden Raisin Bread

*Oat flour and whole wheat flour combined give this
tender bread a wonderful, whole-grain flavor.*

Makes 12 servings

3/4	cup oat flour (see directions on page 8)
1	cup whole wheat flour
2-1/2	teaspoons baking powder
1	teaspoon ground cinnamon
1/2	cup raisins
2	egg whites
2	tablespoons vegetable oil
2	tablespoons honey
1-1/4	cups skim milk

Topping:

1	teaspoon sugar
1/4	teaspoon ground cinnamon

Preheat oven to 350°.

Lightly oil a 4 x 8-inch loaf pan or spray with a nonstick cooking spray.

In a large bowl, combine both types of flour, baking powder, and cinnamon. Mix well. Add raisins.

In another bowl, combine remaining ingredients. Beat with a fork or wire whisk until blended. Add to dry mixture, mixing until all ingredients are moistened.

Place mixture in prepared pan. Combine topping ingredients and sprinkle evenly over top of bread.

Bake 35 to 40 minutes, until a toothpick inserted in the center of the bread comes out clean.

Cool in pan 5 minutes, then transfer to a rack to finish cooling.

Per serving:

121	Calories
4 g	Protein
3 g	Fat
21 g	Carbohydrate
112 mg	Sodium
1 mg	Cholesterol
2 g	Fiber

Apple–Prune Spice Bread

This spicy bread is a real high-fiber treat.

Makes 12 servings

3/4	cup whole wheat flour
1/2	cup *each* all-purpose flour and oat bran
2	teaspoons baking powder
1/2	teaspoon baking soda
1-1/2	teaspoons ground cinnamon
1/2	teaspoon *each* ground nutmeg and allspice
2	tablespoons vegetable oil
2	egg whites
1/4	cup molasses
1	teaspoon vanilla extract
1	cup skim milk
1/2	cup chopped, pitted prunes (in 1/4-inch pieces)*
1	small, sweet apple, unpeeled, chopped into 1/4-inch pieces (1/2 cup)

Preheat oven to 350°.

Lightly oil a 4 x 8-inch loaf pan or spray with a nonstick cooking spray.

In a large bowl, combine both types of flour, oat bran, baking powder, baking soda, and spices. Mix well.

In another bowl, combine remaining ingredients, *except* prunes and apples. Beat with a fork or wire whisk until blended. Add to dry mixture, along with prunes and apples. Mix until all ingredients are moistened. Place mixture in prepared pan.

Bake 35 to 40 minutes until a toothpick inserted in the center of the bread comes out clean.

Cool in pan 5 minutes, then transfer to a rack to finish cooling.

*An easy way to chop dried fruit is to snip it with kitchen shears.

Per serving:

127	Calories
4 g	Protein
3 g	Fat
22 g	Carbohydrate
126 mg	Sodium
0 mg	Cholesterol
2 g	Fiber

Pumpkin Oat Bread

The cool, rich color and spicy flavor of this delicious
bread make it a must *for holiday entertaining.*

Makes 12 servings

1	cup whole wheat flour
3/4	cup rolled oats
2	teaspoons baking powder
1/2	teaspoon baking soda
1	teaspoon ground cinnamon
1/4	teaspoon ground cloves
1/4	cup firmly packed brown sugar
2	egg whites
2	tablespoons vegetable oil
1/2	cup orange juice (unsweetened)
1	teaspoon vanilla extract
1	cup canned pumpkin

Topping:

1	tablespoon rolled oats
1/4	teaspoon ground cinnamon
1/2	teaspoon sugar

Preheat oven to 350°.

Lightly oil a 4 x 8-inch loaf pan or spray with a nonstick cooking spray.

In a large bowl, combine flour, oats, baking powder, baking soda, cinnamon, cloves, and brown sugar. Mix well.

In another bowl, combine remaining bread ingredients. Beat with a fork or wire whisk until well blended. Add to dry mixture, mixing until all ingredients are moistened.

Place mixture in prepared pan.

Combine topping ingredients and sprinkle evenly over the top of the bread.

Bake 45 to 50 minutes, until a toothpick inserted in the center of the bread comes out clean.

Cool in pan 5 minutes, then transfer to a rack to finish cooling.

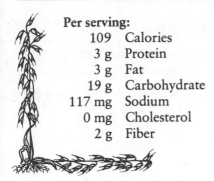

Per serving:

109	Calories
3 g	Protein
3 g	Fat
19 g	Carbohydrate
117 mg	Sodium
0 mg	Cholesterol
2 g	Fiber

Raisin Oat Round

This large, flat loaf is one of our favorites. It's full of raisins and goes well with everything.

Makes 16 servings

1-1/2 cups all-purpose flour
1   cup whole wheat flour
1/2   cup oat bran
1   cup rolled oats
1   tablespoon plus 1 teaspoon baking powder
1/2   teaspoon salt
2/3   cup raisins
2   egg whites
1/4   cup honey
1/4   cup plus 2 tablespoons vegetable oil
1-1/2 cups skim milk

Preheat oven to 350°.

Lightly oil a large baking sheet or spray with a nonstick cooking spray.

In a large bowl, combine dry ingredients. Mix well. Stir in raisins.

In another bowl, combine remaining ingredients. Beat with a fork or wire whisk until blended. Add to dry mixture, mixing until all ingredients are moistened.

Place dough on prepared baking sheet. Shape into a round loaf, 7 or 8 inches in diameter, wetting your hands slightly to keep dough from sticking.

Bake 35 minutes, until bottom of bread is lightly browned. (Bread will spread to about 10 inches in diameter.)

Remove bread from pan, wrap it in a kitchen towel, and place on a rack to cool. (Wrapping the bread in a towel seals in the steam and creates a wonderful texture.)

Per serving:

188	Calories
5 g	Protein
6 g	Fat
30 g	Carbohydrate
194 mg	Sodium
0 mg	Cholesterol
3 g	Fiber

Chili Cornbread

Green chilies and onions dot this bread with color and flavor.

Makes 12 servings

1/4	cup whole wheat flour
3/4	cup oat bran
3/4	cup yellow cornmeal
2	tablespoons sugar
1	tablespoon baking powder
1/2	teaspoon baking soda
1/8	teaspoon salt
1/2	teaspoon chili powder
1/4	teaspoon ground cumin
1	cup skim milk
1	tablespoon lemon juice
2	egg whites
3	tablespoons vegetable oil
1	4-ounce can chopped green chilies, drained
3	tablespoons chopped green onion (green part only)

Preheat oven to 375°.

Lightly oil an 8-inch square baking pan or spray with a nonstick cooking spray.

In a large bowl, combine dry ingredients. Mix well.

Place milk in a small bowl and add lemon juice. Let stand 1 minute. Add egg whites and oil. Beat with a fork or wire whisk until blended. Add to dry mixture, along with chilies and onions, mixing just until all ingredients are moistened. Place batter in prepared pan.

Bake 20 to 25 minutes, until center of bread is firm to the touch and a toothpick inserted in the center comes out clean.

Cool in pan on wire rack. Serve warm for best flavor.

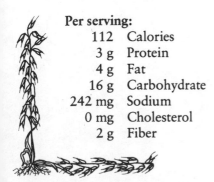

Per serving:

112	Calories
3 g	Protein
4 g	Fat
16 g	Carbohydrate
242 mg	Sodium
0 mg	Cholesterol
2 g	Fiber

Cheesy "Breadwiches"

A layer of cheese in the center, flavored with chives and bacon bits, makes this moist multigrain bread a real hit.

Makes 12 servings

2/3	cup oat bran
2/3	cup whole wheat flour
1/3	cup yellow cornmeal
1/4	cup wheat germ
2	teaspoons baking powder
1	teaspoon baking soda
1/2	cup nonfat dry milk
2	cups water
3	tablespoons vegetable oil
3/4	cup shredded low-fat Cheddar cheese
1	teaspoon dried chives
1	teaspoon imitation bacon bits

Preheat oven to 350°.

Lightly oil an 8-inch square baking pan or spray with a nonstick cooking spray.

In a medium bowl, combine dry ingredients. Mix well. Add water and oil. Beat with a fork or wire whisk until all ingredients are moistened. (Batter may be lumpy.)

Spread half of the batter in prepared pan. Sprinkle cheese gently over dough. Top with chives and bacon bits. Spoon remaining batter over cheese layer.

Bake 30 minutes, until top is set and lightly browned. Let stand 5 minutes before cutting into squares.

Serve hot.

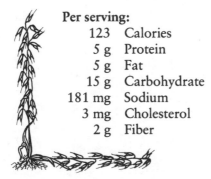

Per serving:

123	Calories
5 g	Protein
5 g	Fat
15 g	Carbohydrate
181 mg	Sodium
3 mg	Cholesterol
2 g	Fiber

Toaster Oat Bread

The "oaty" flavor of this heavy, crusty bread is really enhanced by toasting. You'll love it with soup or chili.

Makes 14 servings

1   cup whole wheat flour
1   cup all-purpose flour
1   cup oat bran
1   cup rolled oats
2   teaspoons baking powder
1   teaspoon baking soda
1/4   teaspoon salt
1   tablespoon lemon juice
2   cups skim milk
1   tablespoon honey

Preheat oven to 375°.

Lightly oil a 5 x 9-inch loaf pan or spray with a nonstick cooking spray.

In a large bowl, combine dry ingredients, mixing well.

In a small bowl, combine lemon juice and milk and let stand 1 minute. Stir in honey and add to dry mixture, stirring until all ingredients are moistened.

Place mixture in prepared pan. Smooth the top lightly with the back of a spoon.

Bake 35 minutes, until crusty and brown, and a toothpick inserted in the center of the bread comes out clean.

Remove to a rack to cool.

Cool completely, then slice and toast.

Per serving:
    124   Calories
     5 g   Protein
     1 g   Fat
    23 g   Carbohydrate
   178 mg Sodium
     1 mg Cholesterol
     3 g   Fiber

Skillet Onion Bread

This onion-topped skillet bread is so quick and easy.
Serve it warm for a moist, chewy texture that can't be
beat.

Makes 8 servings

1/2	cup whole wheat flour
1/2	cup all-purpose flour
1/2	cup oat bran
1	teaspoon baking powder
1/2	tespoon salt
3/4	cup plus 1 tablespoon water
1	tablespoon plus 1 teaspoon margarine, melted
	Poppy seeds
1/3	cup finely chopped onions

Preheat oven to 400°.

Lightly oil a 10-inch cast iron skillet or spray with a nonstick cooking spray.

In a large bowl, combine dry ingredients, mixing well. Add water. Stir until all ingredients are moistened.

Place dough in prepared skillet. Press in pan, wetting your hands slightly to avoid sticking.

Spread margarine evenly over dough. Sprinkle lightly with poppy seeds.

Spread onions evenly over dough, pressing them in slightly.

Bake 25 minutes, until lightly browned.

Cut into 8 wedges and serve hot right from skillet or transfer onto a serving plate.

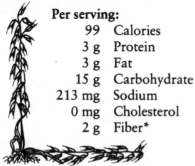

Per serving:

99	Calories
3 g	Protein
3 g	Fat
15 g	Carbohydrate
213 mg	Sodium
0 mg	Cholesterol
2 g	Fiber*

*Fiber is greater than number given. Data is not available for poppy seeds.

Onion 'n Oat Beer Bread

Onions, garlic, and oat bran give this easy favorite a
brand new twist. It's tender, moist, and full of flavor.

Makes 12 servings

3/4   cup whole wheat flour
3/4   cup all-purpose flour
3/4   cup oat bran
2-1/2   teaspoons baking powder
1/4   teaspoon salt
2   tablespoons sugar
1/8   teaspoon garlic powder
1   tablespoon plus 1 teaspoon minced onion flakes
1   12-ounce can light beer (1-1/2 cups), at room temperature
1   tablespoon rolled oats

Preheat over to 375°.

Lightly oil a 4 x 8-inch loaf pan or spray with a nonstick cooking spray.

In a large bowl, combine all ingredients, *except* beer and rolled oats. Mix well.

Add beer, stirring until foam subsides and all ingredients are moistened.

Place mixture in prepared pan. Sprinkle with rolled oats.

Bake 40 minutes, until lightly browned.

Remove bread to a rack to cool.

Per serving:

87	Calories
3 g	Protein
1 g	Fat
18 g	Carbohydrate
135 mg	Sodium
0 mg	Cholesterol
2 g	Fiber

Three-Seed Bread

Toasting brings out the subtle flavor of this bread. The combination of three kinds of seeds and a little honey gives it a taste that will enhance your favorite sandwich filling.

Makes 12 servings

1-1/4 cups whole wheat flour
1/2   cup oat bran
2   teaspoons baking powder
1/4   cup sunflower seeds (unsalted)
2   tablespoons sesame seeds
1   tablespoon poppy seeds
1-1/4 cups skim milk
2   tablespoons vegetable oil
2   tablespoons honey
2   egg whites

Preheat oven to 350°.

Lightly oil a 4 x 8-inch loaf pan or spray with a nonstick cooking spray.

In a large bowl, combine flour, oat bran, baking powder, and seeds. Mix well.

In a small bowl, combine remaining ingredients. Beat with a fork or wire whisk until blended. Add to dry mixture, stirring until all ingredients are moistened.

Place mixture in prepared pan. Smooth the top lightly with the back of a spoon.

Bake 35 to 40 minutes, until a toothpick inserted in the center of the bread comes out clean.

Cool in pan 5 minutes, then invert onto a rack to finish cooling.

Per serving:

128	Calories
5 g	Protein
5 g	Fat
16 g	Carbohydrate
94 mg	Sodium
1 mg	Cholesterol
2 g	Fiber*

*Fiber is greater than number given. Data is not available for seeds.

Yeast Breads

Auntie
Stell's
Grape Jelly

There's nothing like the aroma of a yeast bread baking in the oven to awaken the taste buds and evoke a feeling of warmth. It was a delicious and easy task to add oats to some of my favorite yeast bread recipes and add a new-found nutrition to these wonderful breads.

If bread baking is new to you, here are some helpful hints that will simplify the process:

- Store yeast in the refrigerator but remove it and allow it to come to room temperature before using.
- To dissolve yeast, sprinkle it into lukewarm water, between 105° and 115°.
- Add a small amount of sweetener to the water to speed the growth of the yeast.
- Knead the dough by pushing forward and down, folding the dough back and repeating this rhythm for as long as the recipe specifies.
- While kneading, add only enough flour to keep the dough from sticking.
- Dough should be set to rise in an oiled bowl, and the surface of the dough should be lightly oiled to prevent drying. If you prefer, a nonstick cooking spray can be used for both of these tasks.
- To allow the dough to rise, cover the bowl with a damp towel and place it in a warm spot. An oven with a pilot light will work, or preheat your oven on the lowest possible setting, put the dough in, and turn off the oven.
- The first rising usually takes 1 hour. At this time, the dough should be double its size.
- To punch the dough down, hit it firmly in the center with your fist. This punches out the air.
- If using glass pans, reduce the oven temperature by 25°.
- If you are baking 2 loaves at a time, be sure to leave a space between the pans to allow the heat to circulate.
- Bread is done if it has an even, golden color and sounds hollow when tapped. Testing with a toothpick will not work with yeast breads.

Multigrain Bread

*This bread has a wonderful texture and flavor that makes
it a perfect accompaniment to a steamy hot bowl of soup.
Look for rye flour in any health food store.*

Makes 14 servings

3/4	cup all-purpose flour
3/4	cup whole wheat flour
1/2	cup rye flour
1/2	cup oat bran
1/4	cup yellow cornmeal
1/2	teaspoon salt
1	package active dry yeast
1	cup lukewarm water (105° to 115°)
1/4	cup molasses
2	tablespoons vegetable oil
1	tablespoon rolled oats

Lightly oil a 5 x 9-inch loaf pan or spray with a nonstick cooking
spray.

In a large bowl, combine all three types of flour, oat bran, cornmeal, and salt. Mix well.

Stir 1 teaspoon of the molasses into the lukewarm water in a
small bowl. Sprinkle with the yeast. Let stand 5 minutes.

Stir remaining molasses and oil into the yeast mixture. Add to
flour, mixing with a wooden spoon, and then with your hands, until
all flour is incorporated into the dough.

Place dough in a large oiled bowl and brush the top surface of the
dough lightly with oil. (Both the bowl and the dough can be sprayed
with a nonstick cooking spray, if you prefer.) Cover the bowl with a
damp towel and put in a warm place for 1 hour to rise.

Punch the dough down and turn it onto a lightly floured surface.
(Use all-purpose flour.) Knead about 40 times, adding flour to the
surface as needed to keep dough from being sticky.

Place dough in prepared pan and pat it into the shape of a loaf.
Sprinkle with rolled oats.

Cover pan with the damp towel and put in a warm place to rise
once more, for 1/2 hour.

Preheat oven to 350°.

Bake bread 35 minutes, until top is brown and bread sounds hollow when tapped.

Remove bread to a rack to cool.

Per serving:
- 112 Calories
- 3 g Protein
- 2 g Fat
- 20 g Carbohydrate
- 80 mg Sodium
- 0 mg Cholestereol
- 2 g Fiber

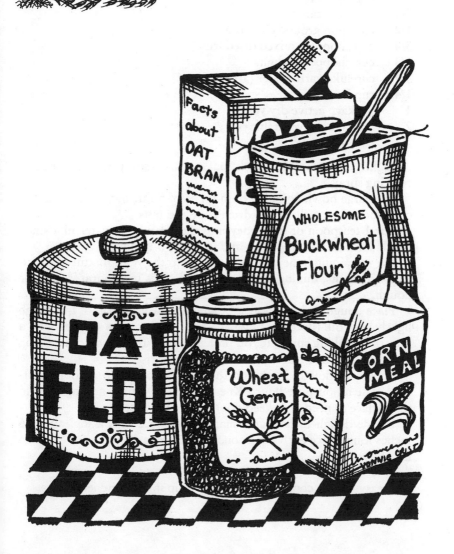

Oatmeal, Fruit and Nut Bread

This recipe makes two wonderful loaves—each chock full of fruits and nuts. For holidays or brunches, they can't be beat.

Makes 2 loaves (12 servings each loaf)

1-1/2	cups whole wheat flour
1-1/4	cups all-purpose flour
1	cup rolled oats
1/4	cup oat bran
1/2	teaspoon ground cinnamon
3/4	cup chopped, mixed dried fruit*
1/3	cup chopped walnuts
3/4	cup lukewarm water (105° to 115°)
1/4	cup honey
1	package active dry yeast
2	tablespoons vegetable oil
1	cup skim milk

Lightly oil two 4 x 8-inch loaf pans or spray with a nonstick cooking spray.

In a large bowl, combine both types of flour, oats, oat bran, and cinnamon. Mix well. Stir in dried fruit and nuts.

Stir 1 teaspoon of the honey into the lukewarm water in a small bowl. Sprinkle with the yeast and let stand 5 minutes.

Stir remaining honey, oil, and milk into the yeast mixture. Add to dry ingredients, mixing until all of the flour is incorporated into the dough.

Place dough in a large oiled bowl and brush the top of the dough lightly with oil. (Both the bowl and the dough can be sprayed with a nonstick cooking spray, if you prefer.) Cover the bowl with a damp towel and put in a warm place for 1 hour to rise.

Punch the dough down and then turn it out onto a floured surface. (Use all-purpose flour.) Knead about 30 times, adding flour to the surface as needed to keep dough from being sticky.

Divide dough in half and shape each piece into a log, about 6 inches long. Place each log in one of the prepared pans and pat into the shape of a loaf.

*An easy way to chop dried fruit is to snip it with kitchen shears.

Cover pans with the damp towel and put in a warm place to rise once more, for 1/2 hour.

Preheat oven to 350°.

Bake loaves 35 minutes, until tops are golden brown and breads sound hollow when tapped.

Remove breads to a rack to cool.

Per serving:

225	Calories
6 g	Protein
5 g	Fat
40 g	Carbohydrate
14 mg	Sodium
0 mg	Cholesterol
4 g	Fiber

Steel-Cut Sandwich Loaf

This is one of our favorite sandwich breads. It's soft,
moist, and sweet, with bits of oats throughout.

Makes 12 servings

1/2	cup steel-cut oats
3/4	cup boiling water
1	cup whole wheat flour
1	cup all-purpose flour
1/4	cup nonfat dry milk
1/4	cup lukewarm water (105° to 115°)
1/4	cup honey
1	package active dry yeast
2	tablespoons vegetable oil

Lightly oil a 4 x 8-inch loaf pan or spray with a nonstick cooking spray.

Pour boiling water over oats in a small bowl. Set aside and cool to lukewarm.

In a large bowl, combine both types of flour and dry milk. Mix well.

Stir 1 teaspoon of the honey into the 1/4 cup of lukewarm water in a small bowl and sprinkle with the yeast. Let stand 5 minutes.

Stir remaining honey and oil into yeast mixture. Stir into lukewarm oats. Add to dry ingredients, mixing with a spoon, and then with your hands, until all of the flour is incorporated into the dough.

Place dough in a large oiled bowl and brush the top of the dough lightly with oil. (Both the bowl and the dough can be sprayed with a nonstick cooking spray, if you prefer.) Cover the bowl with a damp towel and put in a warm place for 1 hour to rise.

Punch the dough down and then turn it out onto a floured surface. (Use all-purpose flour.) Knead for 3 minutes, adding flour to the surface as needed to keep dough from being sticky.

Place dough in prepared pan and pat it into the shape of a loaf. Lightly oil (or spray) the top of the bread.

Cover with the damp towel and put in a warm place to rise once more, for 30 minutes.

Preheat oven to 350°.

Bake bread 35 minutes, until top is brown and bread sounds hollow when tapped.

Remove bread to a rack to cool.

Per serving:
- 148 Calories
- 4 g Protein
- 3 g Fat
- 27 g Carbohydrate
- 9 mg Sodium
- 0 mg Cholesterol
- 3 g Fiber

Orange Raisin Bread

Toasting this bread really *brings out the wonderful orange flavor.*

Makes 12 servings

1	cup whole wheat flour
3/4	cup all-purpose flour
3/4	cup oat bran
1/3	cup raisins
1/4	cup lukewarm water (105° to 115°)
1/4	cup honey
1	package active dry yeast
1/2	cup orange juice (unsweetened)
2	tablespoons vegetable oil
1	teaspoon grated fresh orange peel

Lightly oil a 4 x 8-inch loaf pan or spray with a nonstick cooking spray.

In a large bowl, combine both types of flour and oat bran. Mix well. Stir in raisins.

Stir 1 teaspoon of the honey into the lukewarm water in a small bowl and sprinkle with the yeast. Let stand 5 minutes.

Stir remaining honey, orange juice, oil, and orange peel into yeast mixture. Add to dry ingredients, mixing until all of the flour is incorporated into the dough.

Place dough in a large oiled bowl and brush the top of the dough lightly with oil. (Both the bowl and the dough can be sprayed with a nonstick cooking spray, if you prefer.) Cover the bowl with a damp towel and put in a warm place for 1 hour to rise.

Punch the dough down and then turn it out onto a floured surface. (Use all-purpose flour.) Knead for 3 minutes, adding flour to the surface as needed to keep dough from being sticky.

Place dough in prepared pan and pat it into the shape of a loaf.

Cover with the damp towel and put in a warm place to rise once more, for 30 minutes.

Preheat oven to 350°.

Bake bread 35 minutes, until top is brown and bread sounds hollow when tapped.

Remove bread to a rack to cool.

Per serving:
- 142 Calories
- 4 g Protein
- 3 g Fat
- 26 g Carbohydrate
- 2 mg Sodium
- 0 mg Cholesterol
- 3 g Fiber

Oatmeal Bread

Rolled oats give this loaf a sweet flavor and a moist, chewy texture. It's great with any of your favorite toppings.

Makes 14 servings

1-1/2 cups rolled oats
1/4   cup oat bran
1-1/2 cups boiling water
1-1/2 cups whole wheat flour
1   cup all-purpose flour
1/4   cup nonfat dry milk
1/4   cup lukewarm water (105° to 115°)
1   package active dry yeast
2   tablespoons plus 1 teaspoon honey
2   tablespoons vegetable oil

Lightly oil a 5 x 9-inch loaf pan or spray with a nonstick cooking spray.

In a large bowl, combine rolled oats and oat bran. Add boiling water and set aside to cool to lukewarm.

In another bowl, combine both types of flour and dry milk. Mix well.

Stir 1 teaspoon of honey into the 1/4 cup of lukewarm water in a small bowl and sprinkle with the yeast. Let stand 5 minutes.

Stir remaining honey and oil into yeast mixture. Stir into lukewarm oats, breaking up large lumps with the spoon.

Add *half* the flour to the oat mixture, mixing with a spoon and then with your hands, until the flour is incorporated into the dough.

Place dough on a lightly floured surface (use all-purpose flour) and knead 5 minutes; gradually add as much of the remaining flour as the dough will hold. (Save flour that is left.)

Place dough in a large oiled bowl and brush the top lightly with oil. (Both the bowl and the dough can be sprayed with a nonstick cooking spray, if you prefer.) Cover the bowl with a damp towel and put in a warm place for 1 hour to rise.

Punch the dough down and turn it out onto floured surface. Knead 5 minutes, gradually adding all remaining flour.

Place dough in prepared pan and pat it into the shape of a loaf.

Cover pan with the damp towel and put it in a warm place to rise once more, for 30 minutes.

Preheat oven to 350°

Bake bread 40 minutes, until top is golden and bread sounds hollow when tapped.

Remove bread to a rack to cool.

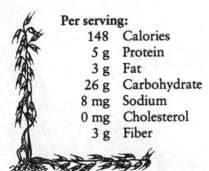

Per serving:

148	Calories
5 g	Protein
3 g	Fat
26 g	Carbohydrate
8 mg	Sodium
0 mg	Cholesterol
3 g	Fiber

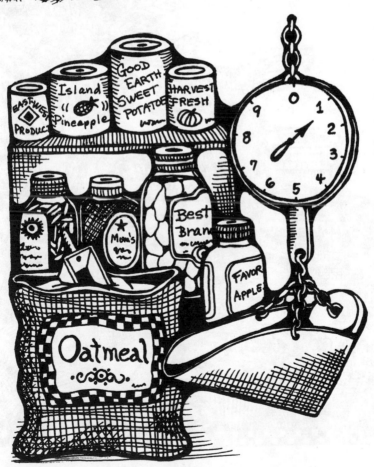

Muffins

Muffins *are definitely making a* comeback in America. Not only are they delicious, but they are so versatile. They're great for breakfast, make a nutritious replacement for cupcakes in lunchboxes, and are delectable desserts. And, whoever said that sandwiches *have* to be made on two slices of bread?

It's easy to add the soluble fiber of oats to muffins. I found that, as with the breads, you can replace approximately one-third of the flour with oat bran or rolled oats.

To sweeten the muffins, I have usually used honey, molasses, or pure maple syrup. I found that by doing this I can greatly reduce the amount of oil in a recipe and still maintain a moist texture. I have used egg whites in place of whole eggs, and, of course, skim milk and other low-fat dairy products.

Not all muffins in this section are sweet. There are a few with herbs and vegetables that make perfect dinner accompaniments. In all of them, I have added lots of high-fiber ingredients, such as fresh or dried fruits, for texture and nutrition that can't be beat.

All muffins in this section were baked in a standard muffin pan, with the cups measuring 3 inches across the top and 1-1/2 inches deep. If you wish to use larger or smaller cups, the baking times may have to be altered.

In most muffin recipes the dry ingredients are mixed together, the liquid ingredients are whisked and added to the dry, and the mixture is stirred just until all ingredients are moistened. Be sure to avoid overmixing, which can toughen the muffins.

I have found that muffins are at their best when eaten the same day, ideally while still warm. However, they reheat nicely in a toaster oven or microwave. After the second day, I always store muffins in the refrigerator (or freezer) because, unlike most commercially baked goods, they contain no preservativees.

Here are some ideas that will help you add the nutrition of oats to your favorite muffin recipes:

- Replace one-fourth to one-third of the flour with oat bran.
- Make a streusel topping of oat bran, wheat germ, and cinnamon.
- Replace one-third to one-half of the cornmeal with oat bran in your favorite corn muffin recipe.
- Substitute oat bran for one-third of the wheat bran in any bran muffin recipe.

Original Oat Bran Muffins

Oat bran is coarser than flour, making oat bran muffins a little dryer than other types of muffins. So we've added lots of raisins and the suggestion that you serve these high-fiber gems warm.

Makes 12 muffins

1/2 cup whole wheat flour
2 cups oat bran
2 teaspoons baking powder
1 teaspoon baking soda
1-1/2 teaspoons ground cinnamon
1/2 cup raisins
3 egg whites
1-1/4 cups skim milk
1/4 cup firmly packed brown sugar
3 tablespoons vegetable oil
1-1/2 teaspoons vanilla extract

Preheat oven to 375°.

Lightly oil 12 muffin cups or spray with a nonstick cooking spray.

In a large bowl, combine flour, oat bran, baking powder, baking soda, and cinnamon. Mix well. Add raisins.

In another bowl, combine remaining ingredients. Beat with a fork or wire whisk until blended. Add to dry mixture, mixing until all ingredients are moistened.

Divide mixture evenly into prepared muffin cups.

Bake 20 minutes, until a toothpick inserted in the center of a muffin comes out clean.

Remove muffins to a rack to cool.

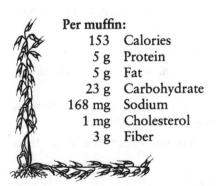

Per muffin:

153	Calories
5 g	Protein
5 g	Fat
23 g	Carbohydrate
168 mg	Sodium
1 mg	Cholesterol
3 g	Fiber

Pineapple Oat Bran Cakes

Unlike ordinary muffins with their rounded tops, these muffins are rather flat. They started out as a "mistake" and became one of our favorites.

Makes 12 muffins

2	cups oat bran
1	tablespoon baking powder
1-1/2	teaspoons ground cinnamon
1/4	cup firmly packed brown sugar
2	egg whites
2	tablespoons vegetable oil
1	cup orange juice (unsweetened)
1	teaspoon vanilla extract
1/4	teaspoon orange extract
1/2	cup canned crushed pineapple (unsweetened), drained

Preheat oven to 375°.

Lightly oil 12 muffin cups or spray with a nonstick cooking spray.

In a large bowl, combine oat bran, baking powder, and cinnamon. Mix well.

In another bowl, combine remaining ingredients, *except* pineapple. Beat with a fork or wire whisk until blended. Add to dry mixture, along with pineapple, mixing until all ingredients are moistened.

Divide mixture evenly into prepared muffin cups.

Bake 25 minutes, until lightly browned.

Remove from pan and cool upside-down on a rack.

Per muffin:

113	Calories
4 g	Protein
4 g	Fat
17 g	Carbohydrate
117 mg	Sodium
0 mg	Cholesterol
2 g	Fiber

Cooked Oat Bran Muffins

What a wonderful way to use leftover cooked oat bran cereal!

Makes 10 muffins

1	cup whole wheat flour
1/2	cup all-purpose flour
1	tablespoon plus 1 teaspoon baking powder
1	teaspoon ground cinnamon
1/3	cup raisins
1	cup cooked oat bran (see cooking instructions, page 3)
1/2	cup skim milk
2	egg whites
2	tablespoons vegetable oil
3	tablespoons firmly packed brown sugar
1	tablespoon vanilla extract

Preheat oven to 375°.

Lightly oil 10 muffin cups or spray with a nonstick cooking spray.

In a large bowl, combine both types of flour, baking powder, and cinnamon. Mix well. Add raisins.

Place cooked oat bran in another bowl and add milk. Beat with a fork or wire whisk until blended. Beat in remaining ingredients. Add to dry mixture. Mix until all ingredients are moistened.

Divide mixture evenly into prepared muffin cups.

Bake 18 to 20 minutes, until a toothpick inserted in the center of a muffin comes out clean.

Remove muffins to a rack to cool.

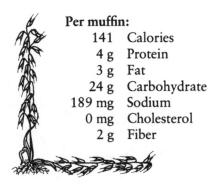

Per muffin:

141	Calories
4 g	Protein
3 g	Fat
24 g	Carbohydrate
189 mg	Sodium
0 mg	Cholesterol
2 g	Fiber

Orange–Pecan–Currant Muffins

These delectable muffins make a wonderful homemade holiday gift. They're a hit with everyone.

Makes 8 muffins

1	cup whole wheat flour
1/2	cup oat bran
1	teaspoon baking soda
1/2	teaspoon baking powder
1/2	teaspoon ground cinnamon
1/4	cup orange juice (unsweetened)
1	cup applesauce (unsweetened)
2	egg whites
2	tablespoons vegetable oil
1-1/2	teaspoons vanilla extract
1	teaspoon grated fresh orange rind
1/4	cup honey
1/4	cup currants or raisins
1/4	cup chopped pecans

Preheat oven to 375°.

Lightly oil 8 muffin cups or spray with a nonstick cooking spray.

In a large bowl, combine dry ingredients. Mix well.

In another bowl, combine remaining ingredients, *except* currants and pecans. Beat with a fork or wire whisk until blended. Add to dry mixture, along with currants and pecans, mixing until all ingredients are moistened.

Divide mixture evenly into prepared muffin cups.

Bake 20 to 23 minutes, until a toothpick inserted in the center of a muffin comes out clean.

Remove muffins to a rack to cool.

Per muffin:

192	Calories
4 g	Protein
6 g	Fat
31 g	Carbohydrate
144 mg	Sodium
0 mg	Cholesterol
4 g	Fiber

Raisin Bran Muffins

High in fiber and high in taste, these are our favorite bran muffins. They combine the soluble fiber of oat bran with the insoluble fiber of wheat bran for a muffin that's doubly good.

Makes 9 muffins

3/4	cup whole wheat flour
3/4	cup wheat bran
3/4	cup oat bran
1-1/2	teaspoons baking soda
1-1/2	teaspoons ground cinnamon
1-1/2	cups skim milk
1	tablespoon lemon juice
2	egg whites
1/4	cup molasses
1	tablespoon vegetable oil
1-1/2	teaspoons vanilla extract
1/3	cup raisins

Preheat oven to 375°.

Lightly oil 9 muffin cups or spray with a nonstick cooking spray.

In a large bowl, combine flour, both types of bran, baking soda, and cinnamon. Mix well.

In a small bowl, combine lemon juice and milk. Let stand 1 minute. Add remaining ingredients, *except* raisins. Beat with a fork or wire whisk until blended. Add to dry mixture, along with raisins, stirring until all ingredients are moistened.

Divide mixture evenly into prepared muffin cups.

Bake 20 minutes, until a toothpick inserted in the center of a muffin comes out clean.

Remove muffins to a rack to cool.

Per muffin:

149	Calories
6 g	Protein
3 g	Fat
26 g	Carbohydrate
172 mg	Sodium
1 mg	Cholesterol
4 g	Fiber

Pineapple Yogurt Muffins

Chunky bits of pineapple, enhanced by the taste of
orange, make these muffins special.

Makes 10 muffins

1-1/2 cups whole wheat flour
1/2   cup oat bran
1   teaspoon baking powder
1/2   teaspoon baking soda
1-1/2 teaspoons ground cinnamon
1/4   teaspoon ground nutmeg
1/3   cup firmly packed brown sugar
1   cup plain nonfat yogurt
1/4   cup water
2   tablespoons vegetable oil
2   egg whites
1-1/2 teaspoons vanilla extract
1   teaspoon grated fresh orange rind
1   cup canned crushed pineapple (unsweetened), drained well

Preheat oven to 375°.

Lightly oil 10 muffin cups or spray with a nonstick cooking spray.

In a large bowl, combine flour, oat bran, baking powder, baking soda, and spices. Mix well.

In another bowl, combine remaining ingredients, *except* pineapple. Beat with a fork or wire whisk until blended. Stir in pineapple. Add to dry mixture. Mix until all ingredients are moistened.

Divide mixture evenly into prepared muffin cups.

Bake 18 to 20 minutes, until a toothpick inserted in the center of a muffin comes out clean.

Remove muffins to a rack to cool.

Per muffin:

162	Calories
5 g	Protein
4 g	Fat
29 g	Carbohydrate
114 mg	Sodium
0 mg	Cholesterol
3 g	Fiber

Cherry–Almond Oat Muffins

The almond flavor really complements the cherries in these moist, chewy muffins.

Makes 8 muffins

1/2	cup whole wheat flour
1/2	cup all-purpose flour
3/4	cup rolled oats
1	teaspoon baking powder
1/2	teaspoon baking soda
2	tablespoons vegetable oil
2	egg whites
1/4	cup sugar
3/4	cup skim milk
1	teaspoon vanilla extract
1	teaspoon almond extract
1	cup frozen, dark sweet cherries, cut in half (do not thaw)

Preheat oven to 375°.

Lightly oil 8 muffin cups or spray with a nonstick cooking spray.

In a large bowl, combine both types of flour, oats, baking powder, and baking soda. Mix well.

In another bowl, combine remaining ingredients, *except* cherries. Beat with a fork or wire whisk until blended. Add to dry mixture, along with cherries. Mix until all ingredients are moistened.

Divide mixture evenly into prepared muffin cups.

Bake 15 to 20 minutes, until a toothpick inserted in the center of a muffin comes out clean.

Remove muffins to a rack to cool.

Per muffin:

166	Calories
5 g	Protein
4 g	Fat
27 g	Carbohydrate
130 mg	Sodium
0 mg	Cholesterol
2 g	Fiber

Raspberry Muffins

These tender muffins have a wonderful, subtle berry flavor, and the sweeter the raspberries, the sweeter the muffins.

Makes 8 muffins

1	cup whole wheat flour
1/2	cup oat bran
2	teaspoons baking powder
2-1/2	cups raspberries, fresh or frozen (if frozen, use unsweetened berries and thaw before using)
1/4	cup skim milk
2	egg whites
2	tablespoons vegetable oil
1-1/2	teaspoons vanilla extract
1/4	cup honey

Preheat oven to 375°.

Lightly oil 8 muffin cups or spray with a nonstick cooking spray.

In a large bowl, combine flour, oat bran, and baking powder. Mix well.

Place raspberries in a blender container and blend until smooth. Press through a strainer, discarding seeds. Add water to pureed berries, if necessary, to equal 1 cup. Add remaining ingredients to berries. Beat with a fork or wire whisk until blended. Add to dry mixture, stirring until all ingredients are moistened.

Divide mixture evenly into prepared muffin cups.

Bake 20 to 23 minutes, until a toothpick inserted in the center of a muffin comes out clean.

Remove muffins to a rack to cool.

Per muffin:

162	Calories
5 g	Protein
4 g	Fat
28 g	Carbohydrate
124 mg	Sodium
0 mg	Cholesterol
4 g	Fiber

Cinnamon Fig Muffins

The flavor of cinnamon and the subtle crunch of fig seeds make these high-fiber muffins uniquely special.

Makes 8 muffins

3/4	cup whole wheat flour
1/2	cup all-purpose flour
1/2	cup oat bran
2	teaspoons baking powder
2-1/4	teaspoons ground cinnamon
2/3	cup chopped dried figs*
2	egg whites
2	tablespoons vegetable oil
1/4	cup honey
1	cup plus 2 tablespoons skim milk
1/2	teaspoon grated fresh orange peel
1	teaspoon vanilla extract

Preheat oven to 375°.

Lightly oil 8 muffin cups or spray with a nonstick cooking spray.

In a large bowl, combine both types of flour, oat bran, baking powder, and cinnamon. Mix well. Add dried figs.

In another bowl, combine remaining ingredients. Beat with a fork or wire whisk until blended. Add to dry mixture, mixing until all ingredients are moistened.

Divide mixture evenly into prepared muffin cups.

Bake 20 minutes, until a toothpick inserted in the center of a muffin comes out clean.

Remove to a rack to cool.

*An easy way to chop dried fruit is to snip it with kitchen shears.

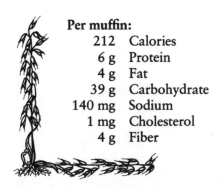

Per muffin:

212	Calories
6 g	Protein
4 g	Fat
39 g	Carbohydrate
140 mg	Sodium
1 mg	Cholesterol
4 g	Fiber

Blueberry Muffins

Everyone loves blueberry muffins! Be sure to freeze plenty of berries in the summer so you can enjoy these delectable treats all year long.

Makes 8 muffins

1/2	cup all-purpose flour
1/2	cup whole wheat flour
1/2	cup oat bran
2	teaspoons baking powder
1/4	cup honey
2	egg whites
2	tablespoons vegetable oil
1/2	cup apple juice
2	teaspoons vanilla extract
1/4	teaspoon lemon extract
1	cup fresh or frozen blueberries (if using frozen berries, do not thaw)

Preheat over to 375°.

Lightly oil 8 muffin cups or spray with a nonstick cooking spray.

In a medium bowl, combine both types of flour, oat bran, and baking powder. Mix well.

In another bowl, combine remaining ingredients, *except* blueberries. Beat with a fork or wire whisk until blended. Add to dry mixture, along with blueberries, stirring until all ingredients are moistened.

Divide mixture evenly into prepared muffin cups.

Bake 20 minutes, until a toothpick inserted in the center of a muffin comes out clean.

Remove muffins to a rack to cool.

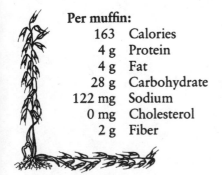

Per muffin:

163	Calories
4 g	Protein
4 g	Fat
28 g	Carbohydrate
122 mg	Sodium
0 mg	Cholesterol
2 g	Fiber

Lemon Pear Muffins

You'll love the lemony taste of these delicious, moist muffins. They make a perfect tea-time treat.

Makes 10 muffins

1-1/4	cups whole wheat flour
1/2	cup oat bran
1	teaspoon baking soda
1	teaspoon ground cinnamon
1/4	teaspoon ground nutmeg
1-1/2	cups skim milk
2	egg whites
1/4	cup plus 1 tablespoon honey
2	tablespoons vegetable oil
1	teaspoon vanilla extract
1/2	teaspoon lemon extract
1	teaspoon grated fresh lemon peel
1	large pear, unpeeled, cut into 1/4-inch pieces (1 cup)

Preheat oven to 375°.

Lightly oil 10 muffin cups or spray with a nonstick cooking spray.

In a large bowl, combine flour, oat bran, baking soda, and spices. Mix well.

In another bowl, combine remaining ingredients, *except* pear. Beat with a fork or wire whisk until blended. Add to dry mixture, along with pear, stirring until all ingredients are moistened.

Divide mixture evenly into prepared muffin cups.

Bake 20 to 22 minutes, until a toothpick inserted in the center of a muffin comes out clean.

Remove muffins to a rack to cool.

Per muffin:

152	Calories
5 g	Protein
4 g	Fat
27 g	Carbohydrate
113 mg	Sodium
1 mg	Cholesterol
3 g	Fiber

Pumpkin Bran Muffins

*The sweet taste of orange and the moistness of pumpkin
make a wonderful combination in these tasty muffins.*

Makes 10 muffins

3/4	cup whole wheat flour
1-1/3	cups wheat bran
1	cup rolled oats
1	teaspoon baking soda
1-1/2	teaspoons ground cinnamon
1/2	teaspoon ground nutmeg
3/4	cup canned pumpkin
1	cup skim milk
1/4	cup pure maple syrup
2	tablespoons vegetable oil
1	teaspoon vanilla extract
1	teaspoon grated fresh orange rind
1/2	cup raisins

Preheat oven to 400°.

Lightly oil 10 muffin cups or spray with a nonstick cooking spray.

In a large bowl, combine dry ingredients. Mix well.

In another bowl, combine remaining ingredients, *except* raisins. Beat with a fork or wire whisk until blended. Add to dry mixture, along with raisins, mixing until all ingredients are moistened.

Divide mixture evenly into prepared muffin cups. Smooth the tops slightly with the back of a spoon.

Bake 20 to 25 minutes, until a toothpick inserted in the center of a muffin comes out clean.

Remove muffins to a rack to cool.

Per muffin:

167	Calories
5 g	Protein
4 g	Fat
30 g	Carbohydrate
99 mg	Sodium
0 mg	Cholesterol
6 g	Fiber

Surprise Tomato Muffins

*No one will believe that the secret ingredient in these
spicy muffins is tomato sauce!*

Makes 8 muffins

3/4	cup whole wheat flour
1/2	cup oat bran
2	teaspoons ground cinnamon
1-1/4	teaspoons ground nutmeg
1-1/2	teaspoons baking powder
1	teaspoon baking soda
1/4	cup honey
3	tablespoons vegetable oil
2	egg whites
1	8-ounce can salt-free (or regular) tomato sauce
1	teaspoon vanilla extract
1/3	cup raisins

Preheat oven to 375°.

Lightly oil 8 muffin cups or spray with a nonstick cooking spray.

In a large bowl, combine dry ingredients. Mix well.

In another bowl, combine remaining ingredients, *except* raisins. Beat with a fork or wire whisk until blended. Add to dry mixture, along with raisins, mixing until all ingredients are moistened.

Divide mixture evenly into prepared muffin cups.

Bake 20 to 23 minutes, until a toothpick inserted in the center of a muffin comes out clean.

Remove muffins to a rack to cool.

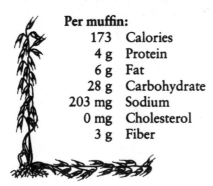

Per muffin:

173	Calories
4 g	Protein
6 g	Fat
28 g	Carbohydrate
203 mg	Sodium
0 mg	Cholesterol
3 g	Fiber

Banana Oat Muffins

The riper the bananas, the sweeter these muffins will be.
They're wonderful warm, spread with peanut butter.

Makes 8 muffins

1	cup whole wheat flour
2	teaspoons baking powder
1/2	teaspoon baking soda
1	cup rolled oats
2	egg whites
1-1/2	teaspoons vanilla extract
1/4	teaspoon almond extract
1/4	cup pure maple syrup
2	tablespoons skim milk
2	tablespoons vegetable oil
1	cup mashed, ripe bananas (about 2 medium bananas)

Preheat oven to 375°.

Lightly oil 8 muffin cups or spray with a nonstick cooking spray.

In a large bowl, combine flour, baking powder, baking soda, and oats. Mix well.

In a small bowl, combine remaining ingredients, *except* bananas. Beat with a fork or wire whisk until smooth. Add mashed bananas. Whisk until blended.

Divide mixture evenly into prepared muffin cups.

Bake 18 minutes, until a toothpick inserted in the center of a muffin comes out clean.

Remove muffins to a rack to cool.

Per muffin:

179	Calories
5 g	Protein
4 g	Fat
31 g	Carbohydrate
174 mg	Sodium
0 mg	Cholesterol
3 g	Fiber

Applesauce Spice Muffins

These tender muffins owe their moistness to the applesauce and their flavor to the wonderful blend of spices. They're really a muffin-lover's dream.

Makes 8 muffins

1	cup whole wheat flour
1/2	cup oat bran
1-1/2	teaspoons baking soda
1	teaspoon ground cinnamon
1/4	teaspoon ground cloves
1/4	teaspoon ground allspice
1/2	teaspoon ground nutmeg
1/4	cup skim milk
2	egg whites
1	cup applesauce (unsweetened)
2	tablespoons vegetable oil
2	teaspoons vanilla extract
1/4	cup molasses
1/4	cup raisins

Preheat oven to 375°.

Lightly oil 8 muffin cups or spray with a nonstick cooking spray.

In a large bowl, combine flour, oat bran, baking soda, and spices. Mix well.

In another bowl, combine remaining ingredients, *except* raisins. Beat with a fork or wire whisk until blended. Add to dry mixture, along with raisins, stirring until all ingredients are moistened.

Divide mixture evenly into prepared muffin cups.

Bake 20 to 23 minutes, until a toothpick inserted in the center of a muffin comes out clean.

Remove muffins to a rack to cool.

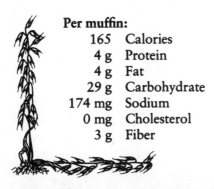

Per muffin:

165	Calories
4 g	Protein
4 g	Fat
29 g	Carbohydrate
174 mg	Sodium
0 mg	Cholesterol
3 g	Fiber

Orange Apricot Muffins

For a variation try dried peaches or pears in place of the apricots in these tasty muffins.

Makes 10 muffins

1	cup whole wheat flour
1/2	cup all-purpose flour
1/2	cup oat bran
1	teaspoon ground cinnamon
1	teaspoon baking powder
1/2	teaspoon baking soda
1/4	cup honey
1	cup orange juice (unsweetened)
3	tablespoons vegetable oil
2	egg whies
1	teaspoon vanilla extract
1	teaspoon grated fresh orange rind
1/2	cup chopped dried apricots*

Preheat oven to 375°.

Lightly oil 10 muffin cups or spray with a nonstick cooking spray.

In a large bowl, combine dry ingredients. Mix well.

In another bowl, combine remaining ingredients, *except* apricots. Beat with a fork or wire whisk until blended. Add to dry mixture, along with apricots, mixing until all ingredients are moistened.

Divide mixture evenly into prepared muffin cups.

Bake 18 to 20 minutes, until a toothpick inserted in the center of a muffin comes out clean.

Remove muffins to a rack to cool.

*An easy way to chop dried fruit is to snip it with kitchen shears.

Per muffin:

174	Calories
4 g	Protein
5 g	Fat
30 g	Carbohydrate
96 mg	Sodium
0 mg	Cholesterol
3 g	Fiber

Jelly Muffins

One of our favorite breakfast treats, these unusual muffins have a burst of flavor in the center. Choose your favorite jam or jelly for the filling.

Makes 8 muffins

1/2	cup whole wheat flour
1/2	cup all-purpose flour
3/4	cup rolled oats
1	teaspoon baking powder
1/2	teaspoon baking soda
2	egg whites
3	tablespoons sugar
3/4	cup skim milk
1-1/2	teaspoons vegetable oil
1/4	cup reduced-sugar or fruit-only jam or jelly, any flavor

Preheat oven to 375°.

Lightly oil 8 muffin cups or spray with a nonstick cooking spray.

In a large bowl, combine both types of flour, oats, baking powder, and baking soda. Mix well.

In another bowl, combine remaining ingredients, *except* jam. Beat with a fork or wire whisk until blended. Add to dry mixture. Mix until all ingredients are moistened.

Using *half* of the batter, divide evenly into prepared muffin cups. Place 1-1/2 teaspoons of jam in the center of each muffin. Top with remaining batter.

Bake 15 to 18 minutes, until lightly browned.

Remove muffins to a rack to cool.

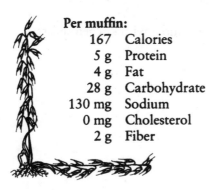

Per muffin:

167	Calories
5 g	Protein
4 g	Fat
28 g	Carbohydrate
130 mg	Sodium
0 mg	Cholesterol
2 g	Fiber

Oat Flour Muffins

*These wheat-free muffins are made entirely with oat flour.
They have a sweet "oaty" taste and a velvety texture all
their own.*

Makes 10 muffins

2	cups oat flour (see directions on page 8)
1	tablespoon baking powder
1/2	cup raisins
1	cup skim milk
1	tablespoon lemon juice
1/3	cup firmly packed brown sugar
2	tablespoons vegetable oil
2	egg whites
2	teaspoons vanilla extract

Preheat oven to 375°.

Lightly oil 10 muffin cups or spray with a nonstick cooking
spray.

In a large bowl, combine flour and baking powder. Mix well. Stir
in raisins.

In a small bowl, combine milk and lemon juice. Let stand 1
minute. Add remaining ingredients. Beat with a fork or wire whisk
until blended. Add to dry mixture, mixing until all ingredients are
moistened.

Divide batter evenly into prepared muffin cups.

Bake 20 minutes, until a toothpick inserted in the center of a
muffin comes out clean.

Remove muffins to a rack to cool.

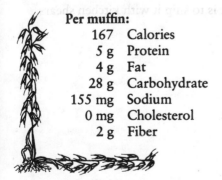

Per muffin:

167	Calories
5 g	Protein
4 g	Fat
28 g	Carbohydrate
155 mg	Sodium
0 mg	Cholesterol
2 g	Fiber

Carob Date Muffins

Oat flour gives these tender muffins the texture of cupcakes and the chewy bits of dates add a tasty surprise to every bite.

Makes 10 muffins

1	cup oat flour (see directions on page 8)
3/4	cup whole wheat flour
1/4	cup carob powder
1	tablespoon baking powder
2/3	cup chopped, dried dates*
2	egg whites
1/4	cup honey
3	tablespoons vegetable oil
1	cup skim milk
1-1/2	teaspoons vanilla extract

Preheat oven to 400°.

Lightly oil 10 muffin cups or spray with a nonstick cooking spray.

In a large bowl, combine both types of flour, carob powder, and baking powder. Mix well. Add chopped dates.

In another bowl, combine remaining ingredients. Beat with a fork or wire whisk until blended. Add to dry mixture, mixing until all ingredients are moistened.

Divide mixture into prepared muffin cups.

Bake 15 minutes, until a toothpick inserted in the center of a muffin comes out clean.

Remove muffins to a rack to cool.

*An easy way to chop dried fruit is to snip it with kitchen shears.

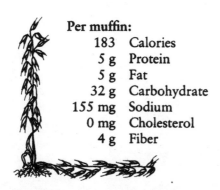

Per muffin:

183	Calories
5 g	Protein
5 g	Fat
32 g	Carbohydrate
155 mg	Sodium
0 mg	Cholesterol
4 g	Fiber

Herbed Corn Cakes

A touch of herbs makes these muffins taste just right.
Serve them warm with dinner or as a delicious brunch
accompaniment.

Makes 8 muffins

3/4	cup whole wheat flour
1	cup rolled oats
2	teaspoons baking powder
1	teaspoon baking soda
1/8	teaspoon dill weed
1/8	teaspoon dried basil
2	teaspoons dried chives
2	egg whites
2	tablesepoons vegetable oil
1	cup cream-style corn
1/4	cup water

Preheat oven to 375°.

Lightly oil 8 muffin cups or spray with a nonstick cooking spray.

In a large bowl, combine flour, oats, baking powder, baking soda, and spices. Mix well.

In another bowl, combine remaining ingredients. Beat with a fork or wire whisk until blended. Add to dry mixture. Mix until all ingredients are moistened.

Divide mixture evenly into prepared muffin cups.

Bake 23 to 25 minutes, until a toothpick inserted in the center of a muffin comes out clean.

Remove muffins to a rack.

Serve warm.

Per muffin:

134	Calories
4 g	Protein
4 g	Fat
21 g	Carbohydrate
314 mg	Sodium
0 mg	Cholesterol
3 g	Fiber

Spinach Muffins

The flavor of spinach, lightly laced with nutmeg and garlic, makes these muffins a perfect accompaniment to your favorite entrée. For a light lunch, try a muffin with a large tossed salad.

Makes 10 muffins

1/2	cup all-purpose flour
3/4	cup whole wheat flour
3/4	cup oat bran
1	teaspoon baking powder
1	teaspoon baking soda
1/4	teaspoon ground nutmeg
1/4	teaspoon garlic powder
1	tablespoon minced onion flakes
2	tablespoons grated Parmesan cheese
2	egg whites
3	tablespoons vegetable oil
1	cup plus 2 tablespoons skim milk
1	10-ounce package frozen, chopped spinach, thawed

Preheat oven to 375°.

Lightly oil 10 muffin cups or spray with a nonstick cooking spray.

In a large bowl, combine both types of flour, oat bran, baking powder, baking soda, spices, onion flakes, and cheese. Mix well.

In another bowl, combine egg whites, oil, and milk. Beat with a fork or wire whisk until blended.

Drain spinach well, squeezing out the water. Stir into egg white mixture. Add to dry mixture, mixing until all ingredients are moistened.

Divide batter evenly into prepared muffin cups.

Bake 18 to 20 minutes, until a toothpick inserted in the center of a muffin comes out clean.

Remove muffins to a rack.

Serve warm.

Per muffin:

140	Calories
6 g	Protein
5 g	Fat
18 g	Carbohydrate
190 mg	Sodium
1 mg	Cholesterol
3 g	Fiber

Cakes and Pies

Cakes *and pies are most* often the center of interest at parties and get-togethers, but, unfortunately, most of them are laden with fats and sugar. So, it became a challenge to create cakes and pies that satisfy a sweet tooth and are still high in fiber and nutrition. I found that adding oat bran and rolled oats to cakes adds a natural sweet flavor and a wonderful texture that really can't be beat. And, adding oats to pie fillings made the fillings thicker and richer than ever.

Like the breads and muffins in this book, I have used honey, molasses, and maple syrup to sweeten most of the cakes and pies. This allowed me to greatly reduce the amount of oil in each recipe and still retain the moistness needed. I have also used unsweetened apple or orange juice as the liquid in many of the recipes, adding even more fat-free moistness. And, to further reduce the fat and cholesterol content of the recipes, I used egg whites in place of whole eggs.

In the cakes and pies in this section that use oil, I use canola oil. Although any vegetable oil will work in a recipe, canola oil is recommended by many health professionals as an oil that is low in saturated fat and high in monounsaturated fat.

Because oven temperatures vary greatly, be sure to check cakes for doneness. A toothpick inserted in the center of the cake will come out clean when the cake is done.

The following are some ideas that will help you incorporate oats and oat bran into your favorite cake recipes:

- Substitute one-fourth to one-third of the flour in a cake recipe with oat bran.
- Use oat bran to replace one-third of the graham cracker crumbs in pie crusts.
- Make a delicious crumb topping by combining oat bran, wheat germ, and cinnamon.
- Replace up to one-third of the flour in a cake recipe with oat flour.
- Add rolled oats or oat bran to your favorite fruit pie filling.
- Use oat bran as a thickener for creamy pie fillings.
- Sprinkle rolled oats over cakes and pies before baking.
- Toast rolled oats in the oven and sprinkle over no-bake pie fillings.

Apple Streusel Cake

Wheat germ, combined with cinnamon and brown sugar, makes a crunchy topping for this moist, apple-filled cake.

Makes 12 servings

1/2	cup whole wheat flour
1/4	cup all-purpose flour
3/4	cup oat bran
1	teaspoon baking soda
1/2	teaspoon baking powder
2	teaspoons ground cinnamon
1/2	teaspoon ground nutmeg
1/4	cup chopped walnuts (optional)
2	egg whites
1	cup applesauce (unsweetened)
2	tablespoons vegetable oil
2	teaspoons vanilla extract
1/3	cup firmly packed brown sugar
1	large, sweet apple, unpeeled, diced into 1/4-inch pieces (1 cup)

Streusel topping:

1	tablespoon firmly packed brown sugar
1	tablespoon wheat germ
1/2	teaspoon ground cinnamon

Preheat oven to 350° (325° for glass pan).

Lightly oil an 8-inch square baking pan or spray with a nonstick cooking spray.

In a large bowl, combine both types of flour, oat bran, baking soda, baking powder, and spices. Mix well. Add chopped nuts.

In another bowl, combine remaining cake ingredients, *except* chopped apple. Beat with a fork or wire whisk until blended. Add to dry mixture, along with apple, mixing until all ingredients are moistened.

Spread batter in prepared pan.

Combine topping ingredients, mixing well. Sprinkle evenly over cake.

Bake 35 minutes, until a toothpick inserted in the center of the cake comes out clean.

Cool in pan on wire rack.

Cut into squares to serve.

Per serving:

117	Calories
3 g	Protein
3 g	Fat
20 g	Carbohydrate
98 mg	Sodium
0 mg	Cholesterol
2 g	Fiber

Harvest Pound Cake

This sensational, moist cake is truly a harvest of fruits and flavors.

Makes 16 servings

1	cup whole wheat flour
1	cup all-purpose flour
1/2	cup oat bran
1/2	cup rolled oats
2	teaspoons baking powder
1	teaspoon baking soda
2	teaspoons ground cinnamon
1	teaspoon ground nutmeg
1/4	cup chopped walnuts
1/2	cup honey
1/4	cup vegetable oil
1	cup apple juice
1	tablespoon vanilla extract
4	egg whites
1	large, sweet apple, unpeeled, cut into 1/4-inch pieces (1 cup)
1	large, ripe pear, unpeeled, cut into 1/4-inch pieces (1 cup)
1/2	cup raisins

Topping:
1-1/2 teaspoons sugar
1/4   teaspoon ground cinnamon

Preheat oven to 350°.

Lightly oil a 10-inch tube pan or spray with a nonstick cooking spray.

In a large bowl, combine both types of flour, oat bran, rolled oats, baking powder, baking soda, cinnamon, nutmeg, and nuts. Mix well.

In another bowl, combine honey, oil, apple juice, vanilla, and egg whites. Beat with a fork or wire whisk until blended. Add to dry ingredients, along with apple, pear, and raisins. Mix until all ingredients are moistened.

Spoon mixture into prepared pan. Combine sugar and cinnamon and sprinkle evenly over the top of the cake.

Bake 45 minutes, until a toothpick inserted in the center of the cake comes out clean.

Cool in pan 5 minutes; remove to a wire rack to finish cooling.

Per serving:

189	Calories
4 g	Protein
5 g	Fat
33 g	Carbohydrate
120 mg	Sodium
0 mg	Cholesterol
3 g	Fiber

Sweet Potato Cake

This tender, moist cake makes a great dessert for holiday time or anytime. Raisins or currants can be used in place of the chopped prunes, if you like.

Makes 12 servings

1/2	cup whole wheat flour
1/2	cup all-purpose flour
1	cup rolled oats
1	teaspoon baking powder
1	teaspoon baking soda
1	teaspoon ground cinnamon
1/2	teaspoon ground nutmeg
1/4	teaspoon ground allspice
2	egg whites
3	tablespoons vegetable oil
1/2	cup orange juice (unsweetened)
1/2	cup firmly packed brown sugar
1	teaspoon vanilla extract
1/2	teaspoon orange extract
1	cup finely shredded, peeled sweet potato
1/4	cup chopped prunes*

Topping:

2	teaspoons sugar
1/4	teaspoon ground cinnamon

Preheat oven to 350° (325° for glass pan).

Lightly oil an 8-inch square baking pan or spray with a nonstick cooking spray.

In a large bowl, combine both types of flour, oats, baking powder, baking soda, and spices. Mix well.

In another bowl, combine remaining ingredients, *except* sweet potato and prunes. Beat with a fork or wire whisk until blended. Add to dry mixture, along with sweet potato and prunes. Mix until all ingredients are moistened.

Spread mixture evenly in prepared pan.

Combine topping ingredients and sprinkle evenly over cake.

Bake 35 minutes, until a toothpick inserted in the center of the cake comes out clean.

Cool in pan on a rack. Serve warm for best flavor.

*An easy way to chop dried fruit is to snip it with kitchen shears.

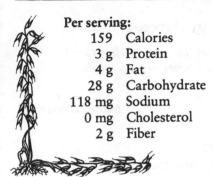

Per serving:

159	Calories
3 g	Protein
4 g	Fat
28 g	Carbohydrate
118 mg	Sodium
0 mg	Cholesterol
2 g	Fiber

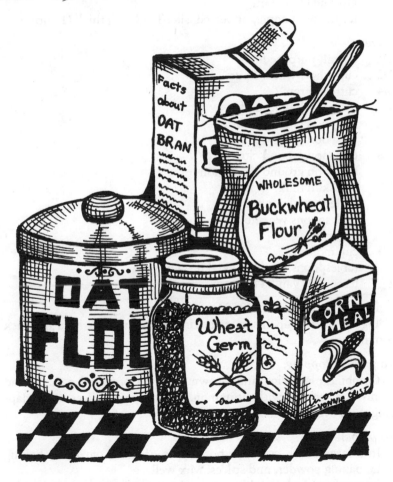

Apple Gingerbread

You'll love the taste of ginger in this moist coffee cake.
For another variation, try sliced pears in place of the
apples.

Makes 12 servings

Topping:

1	tablespoon margarine, melted
1	tablespoon firmly packed brown sugar
	Ground cinnamon
1	large, sweet apple, unpeeled, sliced 1/8 inch thick (1 cup)

Cake:

1/4	cup all-purpose flour
1/2	cup whole wheat flour
3/4	cup oat bran
1	teaspoon baking soda
1/2	teaspoon baking powder
1	teaspoon ground ginger
1/8	teaspoon ground cloves
1	teaspoon ground cinnamon
1	cup skim milk
1	tablespoon lemon juice
3	tablespoons vegetable oil
2	egg whites
1/4	cup molasses
2	tablespoons firmly packed brown sugar
2	teaspoons vanilla extract

Preheat oven to 350° (325° for glass pan).

Lightly oil an 8-inch square baking pan or spray with a nonstick cooking spray.

To prepare topping:

Combine margarine and brown sugar in prepared pan. Spread evenly and sprinkle with cinnamon. Arrange apple slices in overlapping rows over cinnamon.

To prepare cake:

In a large bowl, combine both types of flour, oat bran, baking soda, baking powder, and spices. Mix well.

In another bowl, combine milk and lemon juice and let stand 1 minute. Add remaining ingredients. Beat with a fork or wire whisk until blended. Add to dry mixture, stirring until all ingredients are moistened.

Spread mixture over apples.

Bake 35 to 40 minutes, until a toothpick inserted in the center of the cake comes out clean.

Cool in pan 5 minutes. Then invert onto a rack to cool, or onto serving plate.

Serve warm for best flavor.

Per serving:

134	Calories
3 g	Protein
5 g	Fat
19 g	Carbohydrate
119 mg	Sodium
0 mg	Cholesterol
2 g	Fiber

Festive Fruitcake

*This sensational fruitcake is reminiscent of the rich
holiday cakes, but don't wait for a holiday to try it.*

Makes 16 servings

1-1/2 cups whole wheat flour
1/2   cup all-purpose flour
3/4   cup oat bran
2   teaspoons baking powder
1   teaspoon baking soda
1   teaspoon ground cinnamon
1/4   teaspoon *each* ground nutmeg and allspice
1/8   teaspoon ground cloves
1/3   cup raisins
1-1/2 cups chopped, mixed dried fruit, in 1/4-inch pieces (such as
         apricots, peaches, pears, prunes)*
1/4   cup finely chopped walnuts
1   cup apple juice
1/4   cup *each* honey and molasses
1/4   cup vegetable oil
1/2   cup applesauce (unsweetened)
1   teaspoon vanilla extract
1   teaspoon grated fresh orange peel
4   egg whites

Topping:
2   teaspoons sugar
1/4   teaspoon ground cinnamon

Preheat oven to 350°.

Lightly oil a 10-inch tube pan or spray with a nonstick cooking spray.

In a large bowl, combine dry cake ingredients. Mix well. Stir in raisins, dried fruit, and nuts.

In a medium bowl, combine remaining cake ingredients. Beat with a fork or wire whisk until blended. Add to dry mixture, mixing until all ingredients are moistened. Spoon into prepared pan. Combine topping ingredients and sprinkle evenly over cake.

Bake 45 minutes, until a toothpick inserted in the center of the cake comes out clean.

Cool in pan 5 minutes, then remove to a wire rack to finish cooling.

*An easy way to chop dried fruit is to snip it with kitchen shears.

Per serving:

    201 Calories
      4 g Protein
      5 g Fat
    36 g Carbohydrate
 123 mg Sodium
   0 mg Cholesterol
     3 g Fiber

Banana Ring

*This tender, moist cake has always been a favorite treat in
our house. The riper the bananas, the sweeter the cake.*

Makes 16 servings

3/4	cup whole wheat flour
1/2	cup all-purpose flour
3/4	cup oat bran
1	teaspoon *each* baking soda and baking powder
1/4	cup chopped walnuts (optional)
1/2	cup honey
2	tablespoons vegetable oil
2	egg whites
1/4	cup skim milk
1-1/2	teaspoons vanilla extract
2	medium, very ripe bananas, mashed (1 cup)

Preheat oven to 350°.

Lightly oil a 10-inch tube pan or spray with a nonstick cooking
spray.

In a large bowl, combine both types of flour, oat bran, baking
soda, and baking powder. Mix well. Add nuts.

In another bowl, combine remaining ingredients, *except* mashed
bananas. Beat with a fork or wire whisk until blended. Add bananas
and whisk until mixture is blended. Add to dry mixture, stirring until all ingredients are moistened.

Spoon mixture into prepared pan. Smooth the top of the cake
with the back of a spoon. (Mixture will be shallow in pan.)

Bake 30 minutes, until a toothpick inserted in the center of the
cake comes out clean.

Cool in pan on rack 5 minutes, then remove to a wire rack to
finish cooling.

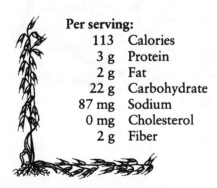

Per serving:
113	Calories
3 g	Protein
2 g	Fat
22 g	Carbohydrate
87 mg	Sodium
0 mg	Cholesterol
2 g	Fiber

Raspberry–Almond Oat Bars

*These chewy, moist cake-like bars make an elegant
dessert that will dress up even the fanciest party.*

Cake: *Makes 12 servings*

2	cups rolled oats
1/4	cup oat bran
1/4	cup firmly packed brown sugar
1	teaspoon baking powder
1	cup apple juice
2	tablespoons vegetable oil
1	teaspoon almond extract
1/2	teaspoon vanilla extract

Topping:

2	tablespoons reduced-sugar or fruit-only raspberry jam
2	tablespoons sliced almonds

Preheat oven to 350° (325° for a glass pan). Lightly oil an 8-inch
square pan or spray with a nonstick cooking spray.

In a large bowl, combine oats, oat bran, brown sugar, and baking
powder. Mix well.

In a small bowl, combine remaining cake ingredients. Add to oat
mixture, mixing until all ingredients are moistened. Let stand 15
minutes.

Stir mixture and spread it in prepared pan. Smooth the top with
the back of a spoon.

Bake 35 minutes, until a toothpick inserted in the center of the
cake comes out clean.

Cool in pan on wire rack.

Spread jam evenly over top of cooled cake. Sprinkle with almonds. Cut into bars to serve.

Per bar:

120	Calories
3 g	Protein
4 g	Fat
19 g	Carbohydrate
38 mg	Sodium
0 mg	Cholesterol
2 g	Fiber

Carob Brownies

These cake-like brownies get their moist texture from
maple syrup and applesauce. You can substitute cocoa for
carob powder, but do try the pleasant, sweet taste of
carob. It tastes somewhat like cocoa and has no caffeine.

Makes 16 servings

Cake:

1/2	cup whole wheat flour
1/4	cup all-purpose flour
3/4	cup oat bran
1/4	cup carob powder
1	teaspoon baking soda
1	teaspoon baking powder
2	egg whites
1/2	cup pure maple syrup
3	tablespoons vegetable oil
1/2	cup apple juice
1/2	cup applesauce (unsweetened)
2	teaspoons vanilla extract
1/4	teaspoon almond extract

Topping:
2-1/2 tablespoons chopped walnuts
2-1/2 tablespoons carob chips (or chocolate chips)

Preheat oven to 350° (325° for a glass pan).

Lightly oil an 8-inch square baking pan or spray with a nonstick cooking spray.

In a large bowl, combine both types of flour, oat bran, carob powder, baking soda, and baking powder. Mix well. In another bowl, combine remaining cake ingredients. Beat with a fork or wire whisk until blended. Add to dry mixture, mixing until all ingredients are moistened.

Place in prepared pan. Sprinkle nuts and carob chips evenly over cake. Press into cake lightly with the back of a spoon.

Bake 40 minutes, until a toothpick inserted in the center of the cake comes out clean.

Cool in pan on wire rack.

Cut into squares to serve.

Per brownie:

112	Calories
2 g	Protein
4 g	Fat
17 g	Carbohydrate
88 mg	Sodium
0 mg	Cholesterol
2 g	Fiber

Pineapple Upside-Down Coffee Cake

An old-time favorite goes healthy!

Makes 12 servings

Topping:

2	tablespoons margarine, melted
2	tablespoons firmly packed brown sugar
1	tablespoon honey
6	slices canned pineapple (unsweetened), drained well
5	blueberries, strawberries or walnut halves (optional)

Cake:

1	cup oat flour (see directions on page 8)
1/2	cup whole wheat flour
1/2	cup all-purpose flour
1	tablespoon baking powder
2	egg whites
1/4	cup honey
3	tablespoons vegetable oil
1	cup skim milk
2	teaspoons vanilla extract
1/4	teaspoon lemon extract

Preheat oven to 350° (325° for a glass pan).

Lightly oil an 8-inch square baking pan or spray with a nonstick cooking spray.

To prepare topping:

Combine melted margarine, brown sugar, and honey in prepared pan. Mix well and spread evenly. Top with 5 of the pineapple rings, placing 1 ring in each corner of the pan and one in the middle. Cut the sixth ring into quarters and use the pieces to fill in the empty spaces. If desired, place a strawberry, blueberry, or half a walnut in the center of each ring.

To prepare cake:

In a large bowl, combine dry ingredients, mixing well.

In another bowl, combine remaining ingredients. Beat with a fork or wire whisk until blended. Add to dry mixture, mixing until all ingredients are moistened. Spread over pineapple.

Bake 35 minutes, until a toothpick inserted in the center of the cake comes out clean.

Cool in pan 3 minutes, then invert cake onto a rack to finish cooling.

Per serving:

181	Calories
4 g	Protein
6 g	Fat
29 g	Carbohydrate
150 mg	Sodium
0 mg	Cholesterol
2 g	Fiber

Honey Sweet Coffee Cake

Sweetened with honey and spiced with cinnamon, this quick and easy coffee cake has a delightful flavor.

Makes 8 servings

Topping:

1	teaspoon ground cinnamon
1	tablespoon plus 2 teaspoons sugar
2	tablespoons finely chopped walnuts (optional)

Cake:

3/4	cup whole wheat flour
1	cup rolled oats
1/4	cup oat bran
1-1/2	teaspoons baking soda
1	teaspoon baking powder
1	cup skim milk
1	tablespoon lemon juice
1/3	cup honey
2	tablespoons vegetable oil
2	egg whites
2	teaspoons vanilla extract

Preheat oven to 350° (325° for a glass pan).

Lightly oil a 6 x 10-inch baking pan or spray with a nonstick cooking spray.

Combine sugar and cinnamon. Set aside with walnuts.

In a large bowl, combine flour, oats, oat bran, baking soda, and baking powder. Mix well.

In a small bowl, combine milk and lemon juice. Let stand 1 minute. Add remaining cake ingredients. Beat with a fork or wire whisk until blended. Add to dry mixture, mixing until all ingredients are moistened.

Place *half* the cake mixture in prepared pan. Sprinkle with *half* of the sugar and cinnamon and *half* of the nuts. Spoon remaining batter carefully over topping. Sprinkle with remaining sugar and cinnamon and top with remaining nuts.

Bake 25 to 30 minutes, until a toothpick inserted in the center of the cake comes out clean.

Cool in pan on a wire rack.

Serve warm for best flavor.

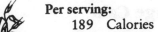

Per serving:

189	Calories
6 g	Protein
5 g	Fat
33 g	Carbohydrate
238 mg	Sodium
1 mg	Cholesterol
3 g	Fiber

Cranberry Orange Cake

Cranberry lovers will flip over the tangy bits of fruit in this moist cake. Be sure to freeze some berries in the Fall so you can enjoy it all year round.

Makes 12 servings

Cake:

1/2	cup whole wheat flour
1/4	cup all-purpose flour
3/4	cup oat bran
1	teaspoon baking powder
1/2	teaspoon baking soda
1	teaspoon ground cinnamon
2	egg whites
1/2	cup honey
3	tablespoons vegetable oil
1/2	cup skim milk
1	teaspoon vanilla extract
1/2	teaspoon orange extract
2	teaspoons grated fresh orange peel
1	cup cranberries

Glaze:

1-1/2	teaspoons softened margarine
2	teaspoons orange juice (unsweetened)
1/4	teaspoon orange extract
1/4	cup confectioners sugar

Preheat oven to 350° (325° for a glass pan).

Lightly oil an 8-inch square baking pan or spray with a nonstick cooking spray.

To *prepare cake:*

In a large bowl, combine both types of flour, oat bran, baking powder, baking soda, and cinnamon. Mix well.

In a blender container, combine remaining ingredients, *except* cranberries. Blend until smooth. Add cranberries and turn blender on and off a few times so that berries will be chopped, rather than pureed.

Add cranberry mixture to dry ingredients, mixing until all ingredients are moistened.

Place mixture in prepared pan. Smooth the top slightly with the back of a spoon.

Bake 30 to 35 minutes, until a toothpick inserted in the center of the cake comes out clean.

Cool in pan on wire rack.

To prepare glaze:

Combine all glaze ingredients. Mix until smooth. Spread on cake after it has cooled 15 minutes.

Cut into squares to serve.

Per serving:
- 149 Calories
- 3 g Protein
- 4 g Fat
- 25 g Carbohydrate
- 90 mg Sodium
- 0 mg Cholesterol
- 2 g Fiber

Carrot Squares

Unlike the typical carrot cake, this one contains no oil at all. Instead, the wonderful, moist texture comes from crushed pineapple and honey.

Makes 12 servings

1/2	cup all-purpose flour
1/2	cup whole wheat flour
1/2	cup oat bran
1	teaspoon baking soda
1	teaspoon baking powder
2	teaspoons ground cinnamon
1/8	teaspoon ground allspice
1/4	cup raisins
3	tablespoons chopped walnuts
1	cup canned crushed pineapple (unsweetened), undrained
2	egg whites
1-1/2	teaspoons vanilla extract
1/2	cup honey
2	cups finely shredded carrots

Preheat oven to 350° (325° for a glass pan).

Lightly oil an 8-inch square baking pan or spray with a nonstick cooking spray.

In a large bowl, combine both types of flour, oat bran, baking soda, baking powder, and spices. Mix well. Add raisins and walnuts.

In a blender container, combine remaining ingredients, *except* carrots. Blend for a few seconds, until mixture is blended, not pureed. Add to dry mixture, along with carrots. Mix until all ingredients are moistened.

Place mixture in prepared pan. Smooth the top slightly with the back of a spoon.

Bake 50 minutes, until a toothpick inserted in the center of the cake comes out clean.

Cool in pan on a rack.

Cut into squares to serve.

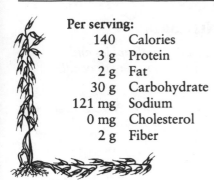

Per serving:

140	Calories
3 g	Protein
2 g	Fat
30 g	Carbohydrate
121 mg	Sodium
0 mg	Cholesterol
2 g	Fiber

Apple–Nut Bars

These delicious cake-like bars, loaded with apples and nuts, just beg to be served warm and topped with vanilla ice milk!

Makes 12 servings

1/2	cup whole wheat flour
1/4	cup oat bran
1	teaspoon baking powder
1	teaspoon ground cinnamon
3	tablespoons chopped walnuts
1/4	cup firmly packed brown sugar
1/2	cup apple juice
1-1/2	teaspoons vanilla extract
1	tablespoon vegetable oil
1	large, sweet apple, unpeeled, chopped into 1/4-inch pieces

Topping:

1-1/2	teaspoons sugar
1/4	teaspoon ground cinnamon.

Preheat oven to 350° (325° for a glass pan).

Lightly oil an 8-inch square baking pan or spray with a nonstick cooking spray.

In a medium bowl, combine flour, oat bran, baking powder, cinnamon, walnuts, and brown sugar. Mix well.

In a small bowl, combine remaining cake ingredients, *except* apple. Add to dry mixture, along with apple. Mix until all ingredients are moistened.

Spread dough in prepared pan.

Combine topping ingredients and sprinkle evenly over cake.

Bake 30 to 35 minutes, until a toothpick inserted in the center of the cake comes out clean.

Cool in pan on a wire rack. Cut into bars to serve.

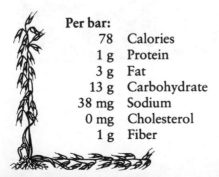

Per bar:

78	Calories
1 g	Protein
3 g	Fat
13 g	Carbohydrate
38 mg	Sodium
0 mg	Cholesterol
1 g	Fiber

Strawberry Jam Bars

These easy, fruity, cake-like bars are sure to become an absolute favorite in your house! They can be made with any flavor jam and taste best when served hot.

Makes 12 bars

3/4   cup whole wheat flour
1   cup rolled oats
1/4   cup oat bran
1/2   teaspoon baking powder
1/4   cup honey
2   tablespoons vegetable oil
1/2   cup apple juice
1   teaspoon vanilla extract
1/3   cup reduced-sugar or fruit-only strawberry jam

Preheat oven to 350°.

Lightly oil an 8-inch square baking pan or spray with a nonstick cooking spray.

In a large bowl, combine flour, oats, oat bran, and baking powder. Mix well.

In a small bowl, combine honey, oil, apple juice, and vanilla. Add to dry mixture, mixing until all ingredients are moistened.

Set aside 1/2 cup of oat mixture. Press remaining mixture firmly in the bottom of prepared pan. (Wet your hands slightly as you work.)

Spread jam evenly over oat mixture.

Using a 1/4-teaspoon measuring spoon, drop remaining mixture evenly over jam. Press down lightly into the jam, again wetting your hands slightly, making a marbled effect.

Bake 20 minutes. Cool in pan on wire rack.

Cut into squares and serve warm for best flavor.

Per bar:
124   Calories
2 g   Protein
3 g   Fat
23 g   Carbohydrate
19 mg Sodium
0 mg   Cholesterol
2 g   Fiber

Lemon Cheese Pie

This pie is so lemony and sweet. They'll love it!

Makes 8 servings

Crust:

1/3	cup oat bran
1/4	cup graham cracker crumbs
1/4	cup wheat germ
1	tablespoon sugar
1/4	teaspoon ground cinnamon
1/4	cup margarine, melted

Filling:

1-1/2	cups low-fat cottage cheese
3	egg whites
1/2	cup sugar
1	tablespoon grated fresh lemon peel
1/4	cup oat bran
1	tablespoon vegetable oil
1	teaspoon vanilla extract
1/4	teaspoon cream of tartar

Preheat oven to 350°.

Very lightly oil a 9-inch pie pan or spray with a nonstick cooking spray.

To prepare crust:

In a small bowl, combine all crust ingredients, *except* margarine. Mix well. Place in prepared pan. Add margarine. Mix until all ingredients are moistened. Press crumbs firmly into bottom of pan and along the sides, forming a crust.

Bake 10 minutes. Cool.

While crust is cooling, *prepare filling*:

In a blender container, combine cottage cheese, *one* of the egg whites, sugar, lemon peel, oat bran, oil, and vanilla. Blend until smooth. Pour into a large bowl.

In a small, deep bowl, beat remaining 2 egg whites on low speed of an electric mixer until frothy. Add cream of tartar and beat on high speed until egg whites are stiff. Add to cheese mixture, folding gently until both mixtures are combined. Pour into pie crust.

Bake 25 minutes, until filling is set and top begins to brown.

Cool slightly, then chill.

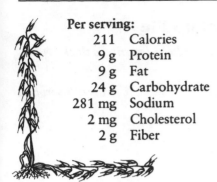

Per serving:

211	Calories
9 g	Protein
9 g	Fat
24 g	Carbohydrate
281 mg	Sodium
2 mg	Cholesterol
2 g	Fiber

Sweet Potato Pie

*This low-fat version of an old Southern favorite is thick
and rich and full of spices.*

Makes 8 servings

Crust:

2/3	cup rolled oats
1/2	cup whole wheat flour
1/2	teaspoon baking powder
1/4	cup plus 1 tablespoon cold skim milk
3	tablespoons vegetable oil

Filling:

1	17-ounce can sweet potatoes, vacuum packed *without* syrup (2-1/2 cups)
1/4	cup oat bran
1	cup orange juice (unsweetened)
2	egg whites
1/2	cup firmly packed brown sugar
1	teaspoon vanilla extract
2	teaspoons ground cinnamon
1/4	teaspoon ground nutmeg
1/4	teaspoon ground ginger
1/4	teaspoon ground cloves

Topping:

1	teaspoon sugar
1/4	teaspoon ground cinnamon

Preheat oven to 350°.

To prepare crust:

Place oats in a blender container and blend until the consistency
of flour. Place in a medium bowl and add flour and baking powder.
Mix well.

With a fork, stir in milk and oil. Work dough into a ball, using
your hands. Roll dough between 2 sheets of wax paper into a 12-
inch circle. Remove top sheet of wax paper and invert crust into a 9-
inch pie pan. Fit crust into pan, leaving an overhang. Carefully remove remaining wax paper. Bend edges of crust under and flute
dough with your fingers or a fork.

To prepare filling:

In a blender container, combine all filling ingredients. Blend until smooth. (Depending on the power of the blender, it may be necessary to blend mixture in 2 batches because it is very thick. If so, mix both batches well in a bowl after blending.) Pour into prepared pie crust.

Combine topping ingredients and sprinkle evenly over top of pie.

Bake 45 to 50 minutes, until filling is set. When crust is as brown as you like, place a piece of aluminum foil loosely over pie to prevent further browning.

Cool pie slightly, then chill.

Per serving:

243	Calories
5 g	Protein
6 g	Fat
43 g	Carbohydrate
81 mg	Sodium
1 mg	Cholesterol
3 g	Fiber

Orange Bean Pie

This sweet, orange-flavored pie gets its smoothness (and added fiber) from beans. No one will ever guess what's in it! (For a delicious pudding, bake the filling in a pie pan without the crust.)

Makes 8 servings

Crust:

2/3	cup rolled oats
1/2	cup whole wheat flour
1/2	teaspoon baking powder
1/4	cup plus 1 tablespoon cold skim milk
3	tablespoons vegetable oil

Filling:

1	1-pound can Great Northern beans, or butter beans, rinsed and drained
1/3	cup oat bran
1/4	cup frozen orange juice concentrate (unsweetened), thawed
1/2	cup firmly packed brown sugar
1	cup skim milk
2	egg whites
1	teaspoon ground cinnamon
1	teaspoon grated fresh orange peel
1	teaspoon vanilla extract

Preheat oven to 350°

To prepare crust:

Place oats in a blender container and blend until the consistency of flour. Place in a medium bowl and add flour and baking powder. Mix well.

With a fork, stir in milk and oil. Work dough into a ball, using your hands. Roll dough between 2 sheets of wax paper into a 12-inch circle. Remove top sheet of wax paper and invert crust into a 9-inch pie pan. Fit crust into pan, leaving an overhang. Carefully remove remaining wax paper. Bend edges of crust under and flute dough with your fingers or a fork.

To prepare filling:

In a blender container, combine all filling ingredients. Blend until smooth. Pour into prepared crust.

Bake 35 to 40 minutes, until filling is set.

Cool slightly on a wire rack, then chill.

Per serving:
- 263 Calories
- 9 g Protein
- 7 g Fat
- 43 g Carbohydrate
- 67 mg Sodium
- 2 mg Cholesterol
- 5 g Fiber

Molasses–Oatmeal Spice Pie

This unusual pie is similar to the Pennsylvania Dutch favorite, shoo-fly pie. Serve it warm, topped with vanilla ice milk, for an unforgettable dessert.

Makes 8 servings

Crust:

2/3   cup rolled oats
1/2   cup whole wheat flour
1/2   teaspoon baking powder
1/4   cup plus 1 tablespoon cold skim milk
3   tablespoons vegetable oil

Filling:

1   cup rolled oats
1/3   cup firmly packed brown sugar
1/4   cup chopped walnuts
1   teaspoon ground cinnamon
1/4   teaspoon ground nutmeg
1/8   teaspoon ground cloves
1/8   teaspoon ground ginger
2   tablespoons vegetable oil
1/4   cup molasses
1   egg white
1-1/2 teaspoons baking soda
1-1/2 cups plus 2 tablespoons hot water

Preheat oven to 350°.

To prepare crust:

Place oats in a blender container and blend until the consistency of flour. Place in a medium bowl and add flour and baking powder. Mix well.

With a fork, stir in milk and oil. Work dough into a ball, using your hands. Roll dough between 2 sheets of wax paper into a 12-inch circle. Remove top sheet of wax paper and fit dough into a 9-inch pie pan, leaving an overhang. Carefully remove remaining wax paper. Bend edges under and flute dough with your fingers or a fork. Prick the bottom and sides of crust about 25 times with a fork.

Bake 10 minutes.

While crust is baking, *prepare filling:*

In a medium bowl, combine oats, brown sugar, walnuts, and spices. Mix well. Add oil and molasses. Mix with a fork until well blended. Place in baked crust.

Place egg white in a small bowl. Add baking soda. Beat with a fork or wire whisk for a few seconds, until just blended. Add hot water. Whisk for about 10 seconds. Pour over oat mixture.

Bake 30 minutes.

To cool, place on wire rack and place a piece of foil loosely over pie.

Serve warm for best flavor.

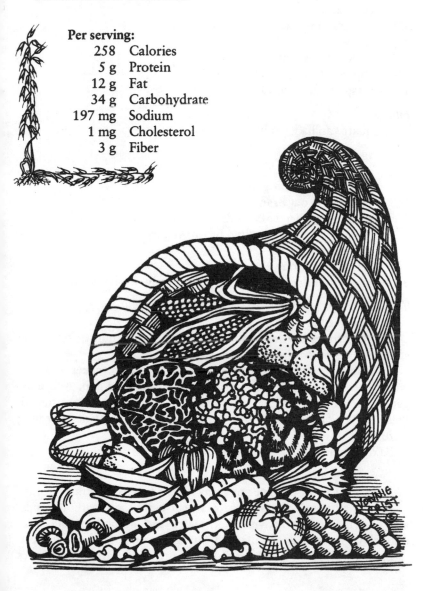

Per serving:
- 258 Calories
- 5 g Protein
- 12 g Fat
- 34 g Carbohydrate
- 197 mg Sodium
- 1 mg Cholesterol
- 3 g Fiber

Party Ice Creme Pie

A very special party pie, this refreshing dessert has a high-fiber crust and a crunchy granola topping.

Makes 8 servings

Crust:
1/3	cup oat bran
1/4	cup graham cracker crumbs
1/4	cup wheat germ
1	tablespoon sugar
1/4	cup margarine, melted
1	teaspoon almond extract

Filling:
1	quart vanilla ice milk

Topping:
2/3	cups rolled oats
1	tablespoon wheat germ
1	tablespoon oat bran
1	tablespoon sliced almonds
1	tablespoon firmly packed brown sugar
3	tablespoons water
1/2	teaspoon almond extract
3	tablespoons reduced-sugar or fruit-only raspberry jam

To prepare crust:

Preheat oven to 350°.

Very lightly oil a 9-inch pie pan or spray with a nonstick cooking spray.

In a small bowl, combine oat bran, graham cracker crumbs, wheat germ, and sugar. Mix well. Place in prepared pan. Add margarine and almond extract. Mix until all ingredients are moistened. Press crumbs firmly into bottom of pan and along the sides, forming a crust.

Bake 10 minutes. Cool completely.

To prepare topping:

Lightly oil a baking sheet or spray with a nonstick cooking spray.

In a small bowl, combine oats, wheat germ, oat bran, almonds, and brown sugar. Mix well. Add water and almond extract. Mix until all ingredients are moistened. Spread on prepared baking sheet.

Bake 10 to 12 minutes, until lightly browned. Stir several times while baking, breaking up any large lumps with the back of a spoon.

Cool on pan.

To prepare filling:

Let ice milk stand at room temperature until softened. Spoon into cooled crust. Smooth the top. Cover with plastic wrap and freeze until firm.

When pie is frozen, spread jam evenly over top. Sprinkle with topping. Cover and return to freezer.

To serve, let stand at room temperature for a few minutes, then cut with a sharp knife that has been dipped in hot water.

Per serving:

252	Calories
6 g	Protein
10 g	Fat
34 g	Carbohydrate
143 mg	Sodium
9 mg	Cholesterol
2 g	Fiber

Pineapple Cheese Pie

*Super-moist and full of pineapple, this pie can't help but
be a hit.*

Makes 8 servings

Crust:
1/3   cup oat bran
1/4   cup graham cracker crumbs
1/4   cup wheat germ
1   tablespoon sugar
1/4   teaspoon ground cinnamon
1/4   cup margarine, melted

Filling:
1-1/2   cups part-skim ricotta cheese
3   egg whites
1/4   cup plus 2 tablespoons sugar
1/4   cup oat bran
1/4   teaspoon lemon extract
1   teaspoon vanilla extract
1   cup canned crushed pineapple (unsweetened), drained

Preheat oven to 350°.

Lightly oil a 9-inch pie pan or spray with a nonstick cooking
spray.

To prepare crust:

In a small bowl, combine all crust ingredients, *except* margarine.
Mix well. Place in prepared pan. Add margarine. Mix until all ingredients are moistened. Press crumbs firmly into bottom of pan and
along the sides, forming a crust.

Bake 10 minutes. Cool.

While crust is cooling, *prepare filling:*

In a blender container, combine all filling ingredients, *except*
pineapple. Blend until smooth. Stir in pineapple. Spoon into crust.

Bake 35 to 40 minutes, until set. Cool slightly, then chill.

Per serving:
    236   Calories
      9 g   Protein
     10 g   Fat
     27 g   Carbohydrate
    167 mg Sodium
     14 mg Cholesterol
      2 g   Fiber

Puddings
and
Crisps

Puddings and crisps are ideal foods to be made with oats. Toppings for fruit crisps have traditionally been made from rolled oats, and many old, old cookbooks use rolled oats in steamed puddings.

In creating recipes for this section, I found that it is easy to make both puddings and crisps with a very small amount of oil. Fruit juice makes a wonderful fat-free oil replacement, as does the use of honey, molasses, or pure maple syrup as a sweetener. Using these ingredients means that less oil can be used, but the finished product will still have the necessary amount of moistness. When recipes call for vegetable oil I use canola oil. Although any vegetable oil will work, canola oil has been recommended by many health professionals because it is low in saturated fat and high in monounsaturated fat, qualities that are believed to help lower blood cholesterol levels.

Following are some helpful hints so that you can create delicious puddings and fruit crisps using the wonderful flavor, texture, and nutrition of oats:

- Use rolled oats for toppings on baked fruit crisps.
- For crisps that do not get baked, toast rolled oats with cinnamon and honey and sprinkle over fruit.
- Use oat bran to replace up to one-third of flour in crisp recipes.
- Make steamed puddings using oat bran or rolled oats in place of some of the flour.
- Put cooked steel-cut oats in the blender with fruit to create "instant" puddings.
- Use cooked whole oats (groats) in place of, or in combination with rice in rice puddings.
- Make cornmeal or spoonbread puddings by replacing up to one-half of the cornmeal with oat bran.

226

Steamed Apple–Oat Pudding

*Surprise them with this spicy, moist pudding for dessert.
Serve it hot, topped with vanilla ice milk, and you'll
definitely have them begging for more. It's also a real
treat for brunch.*

Makes 6 servings

1	cup rolled oats
1/2	teaspoon baking soda
1	teaspoon ground cinnamon
1/2	teaspoon ground nutmeg
1	large, sweet apple, unpeeled, coarsely shredded (1 cup)
3	egg whites
1/3	cup molasses
2/3	cup water
1	tablespoon lemon juice

Preheat oven to 325°.

Lightly oil a 1-quart baking pan or spray with a nonstick cooking spray.

In a large bowl, combine oats, baking soda, cinnamon, and nutmeg. Mix well. Add apple, stirring until evenly distributed.

In a small bowl, combine remaining ingredients. Beat with a fork or wire whisk until blended. Add to oat mixture, mixing well.

Place mixture in prepared pan. Cover tightly with foil. Place in a larger pan and pour enough water in the larger pan to come halfway up the sides of the pan with the pudding.

Bake 1 hour.

Serve warm in pan or let stand 5 minutes and invert onto a serving plate.

Per serving:

119	Calories
4 g	Protein
1 g	Fat
24 g	Carbohydrate
97 mg	Sodium
0 mg	Cholesterol
2 g	Fiber

Indian Pudding

This updated version of the early settlers' traditional Thanksgiving dessert is really special. Too bad they didn't have vanilla ice milk for a topping!

Makes 8 servings

1/4	cup oat bran
1/4	cup yellow cornmeal
1/4	teaspoon baking soda
2	tablespoons firmly packed brown sugar
2	tablespoons vegetable oil
3	cups skim milk
1/4	cup molasses
2	egg whites
1	teaspoon ground cinnamon
1/2	teaspoon ground allspice
1/2	teaspoon ground nutmeg
1/4	teaspoon ground ginger
1	medium, sweet apple, peeled, sliced 1/8 inch thick

Preheat oven to 325°.

Lightly oil an 8-inch square baking pan or spray with a nonstick cooking spray.

In a small saucepan, combine oat bran, cornmeal, baking soda, brown sugar, vegetable oil, and *half* of the milk. Bring to a boil over medium heat, stirring frequently. Remove from heat.

In a medium bowl, combine the rest of the milk with remaining ingredients, *except* apple. Beat with a fork or wire whisk until blended. Add to saucepan, stirring to combine. Stir in apple.

Place mixture in prepared pan.

Bake 1-1/2 hours, uncovered. Serve warm for best flavor.

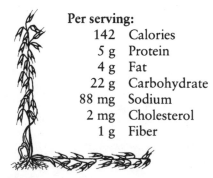

Per serving:

142	Calories
5 g	Protein
4 g	Fat
22 g	Carbohydrate
88 mg	Sodium
2 mg	Cholesterol
1 g	Fiber

Oat Bran Cheese Pudding

Moist and sweet, this cheesy pudding is great either as a dessert or for breakfast.

Makes 8 servings

2	cups water
2/3	cup oat bran
1-1/2	cups low-fat cottage cheese
4	egg whites
1/3	cup skim milk
1/2	cup firmly packed brown sugar
1	teaspoon ground cinnamon
2	teaspoons vanilla extract
1/2	cup raisins

Preheat oven to 325°.

Lightly oil an 8-inch square baking pan or spray with a nonstick cooking spray.

Bring water to a boil in a medium saucepan over medium heat. Add oat bran, stirring briskly with a fork or wire whisk to prevent mixture from forming lumps. Cook 2 minutes, stirring constantly. Remove from heat.

In a blender container, combine remaining ingredients, *except* raisins. Blend until smooth. Add to oat bran, along with raisins. Mix well. Pour mixture into prepared pan. Sprinkle with additional cinnamon.

Bake, uncovered, 45 to 50 minutes, until set.

Cool slightly, then chill. Serve cold.

Per serving:

153	Calories
9 g	Protein
1 g	Fat
27 g	Carbohydrate
208 mg	Sodium
2 mg	Cholesterol
2 g	Fiber

Fruity Oat Pudding

This easy pudding is good hot or cold, with a little skim milk poured over it. Serve it for dessert or as an easy brunch dish.

Makes 6 servings

1-1/2	cups rolled oats
1-1/4	cups orange juice (unsweetened)
1/2	cup applesauce (unsweetened)
1	egg white
1/4	cup raisins
1	teaspoon ground cinnamon
1	teaspoon vanilla extract
1/2	teaspoon almond extract
1/4	cup reduced-calorie or fruit-only raspberry jam

Preheat oven to 350°.

Lightly oil a 1-quart baking pan or spray with a nonstick cooking spray.

In a large bowl, combine all ingredients. Mix well.

Place in prepared pan.

Bake, uncovered, 40 minutes.

Serve hot or cold.

Per serving:

163	Calories
4 g	Protein
1 g	Fat
34 g	Carbohydrate
11 mg	Sodium
0 mg	Cholesterol
3 g	Fiber

Pineapple Oat Pudding

*When you make steel-cut oats for breakfast, make enough
for a batch of this delicious, tapioca-like pudding. It's
good by itself, but for a special dessert, spoon it over
angel food cake and top with sliced strawberries.*

Makes 4 servings

1   cup hot, cooked steel-cut oats (see cooking directions on
         page 7)
1-1/2   cups canned crushed pineapple (unsweetened), undrained
1/2   teaspoon vanilla extract
1/8   teaspoon lemon extract
1   tablespoon plus 1 teaspoon pure maple syrup
1/4   cup nonfat dry milk

In a blender container, combine all ingredients. Blend until
smooth. Place in a serving bowl.
Chill overnight.
Serve cold.

Per serving:
        146   Calories
         4 g Protein
         1 g Fat
        31 g Carbohydrate
        25 mg Sodium
         1 mg Cholesterol
         2 g Fiber

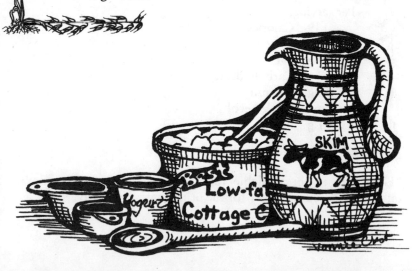

Kasha Apple Pudding

This creamy pudding, with the toasty flavor and aroma of buckwheat, is at its best when served piping hot. Look for kasha in most grocery stores.

Makes 6 servings

1/4	cup kasha (buckwheat groats)
1/3	cup steel-cut oats
1/4	cup plus 2 teaspoons firmly packed brown sugar
1	teaspoon ground cinnamon
1/2	teaspoon *each* ground nutmeg and ginger
2-1/2	cups water
2/3	cup nonfat dry milk
3	egg whites
1	large, sweet apple, unpeeled, chopped into 1/4-inch pieces

Preheat oven to 350°.

Oil a 1-quart baking pan or spray with a nonstick cooking spray.

In a small saucepan, combine kasha, oats, 1/4 cup of the brown sugar, spices, and water. Bring to a boil over medium heat. Boil 1 minute. Remove from heat.

Add dry milk, beating with a fork or wire whisk until blended. Whisk in egg whites. Stir in apple.

Place mixture in prepared pan. Sprinkle with remaining brown sugar. Set in a larger pan and pour enough hot water in the larger pan to come halfway up the sides of the pan with the pudding.

Bake uncovered, 30 to 35 minutes, until set. Serve hot.

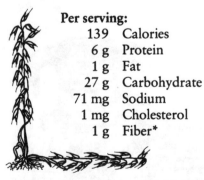

Per serving:

139	Calories
6 g	Protein
1 g	Fat
27 g	Carbohydrate
71 mg	Sodium
1 mg	Cholesterol
1 g	Fiber*

*Fiber data is not available for buckwheat groats. This number reflects the amount of fiber for the other ingredients only.

Creamy Oat Pudding

This creamy dessert or breakfast dish is definitely an oat-lovers' answer to rice pudding.

Makes 6 servings

2	cups skim milk
1/2	teaspoon ground cinnamon
1/4	teaspoon ground nutmeg
1	tablespoon cornstarch
3	tablespoons sugar
2	teaspoons vanilla
2	cups cooked whole oats (groats) (see cooking directions on page 6)
1/4	cup raisins
	Ground cinnamon

Have an ungreased shallow 1-quart baking pan ready.

Place milk in a medium saucepan.

In a small bowl or custard cup, combine cinnamon, nutmeg, and cornstarch. Stir enough of the milk into the cornstarch to dissolve it, then add it to the saucepan.

Add sugar, vanilla, and oats. Cook over medium heat, stirring, until mixture comes to a boil. Continue to cook and stir 3 minutes more.

Remove from heat and stir in raisins.

Pour mixture into pan. Sprinkle with cinnamon.

Chill.

Serve cold.

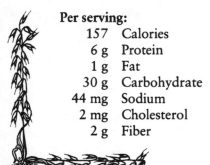

Per serving:

157	Calories
6 g	Protein
1 g	Fat
30 g	Carbohydrate
44 mg	Sodium
2 mg	Cholesterol
2 g	Fiber

Quick Banana Betty

Bananas and granola cereal are combined with orange juice for a super-quick, mouth-watering dessert or breakfast treat.

Makes 4 servings

1   cup granola (page 16)*
1   small, ripe banana, thinly sliced
1   tablespoon chopped walnuts
1   cup orange juice (unsweetened)

Sprinkle *half* of the granola in the bottom of a 1-quart baking dish. Top with sliced banana. Sprinkle with chopped nuts and top with remaining granola.

Spoon orange juice over granola.

Cover and chill several hours or overnight.

Serve cold.

*Commercial granolas will work, but read the labels carefully because many of them are loaded with fat.

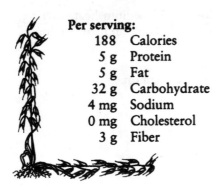

Per serving:
          188   Calories
           5 g   Protein
           5 g   Fat
          32 g   Carbohydrate
           4 mg   Sodium
           0 mg   Cholesterol
           3 g   Fiber

Cherry–Berry Crisp

This crispy delight combines the flavors of cherries and
blueberries for a truly scrumptious dessert.

Makes 8 servings

2	cups frozen, dark sweet cherries (unsweetened)
2	cups blueberries, fresh or frozen
2	tablespoons sugar
2	tablespoons cornstarch

Topping:

2/3	cup rolled oats
1/3	cup graham cracker crumbs
2	tablespoons whole wheat flour
3	tablespoons firmly-packed brown sugar
1	teaspoon ground cinnamon
2	tablespoons nonfat dry milk
1/4	cup vegetable oil
3	tablespoons water

Preheat oven to 350°.

Lightly oil a 9-inch pie pan or spray with a nonstick cooking spray.

In a large bowl, combine cherries, blueberries, sugar, and cornstarch (it is not necessary to thaw fruit, if frozen). Mix well. Place in prepared pan.

To prepare topping:

In a medium bowl, combine oats, graham cracker crumbs, flour, brown sugar, cinnamon, and dry milk. Mix well. Add oil and water. Mix until all ingredients are moistened. Distribute evenly over fruit.

Bake 30 to 35 minutes, until lightly browned.

Serve warm or cold.

Per serving:

202	Calories
3 g	Protein
8 g	Fat
31 g	Carbohydrate
40 mg	Sodium
0 mg	Cholesterol
2 g	Fiber

Pear Crunch

Similar to apple crisp, this delicious dessert tastes best when served warm.

Makes 8 servings

4	ripe, sweet pears, sliced 1/8- to 1/4-inch thick (4 cups)
2	tablespoons apple juice
1	tablespoon lemon juice
1/2	teaspoon ground cinnamon
3	tablespoons firmly packed brown sugar

Topping:

1/2	cup rolled oats
1/2	cup whole wheat flour
1/4	cup Grape Nuts® cereal
1/2	teaspoon ground cinnamon
1	tablespoon firmly packed brown sugar
2	tablespoons vegetable oil
3	tablespoons apple juice

Preheat oven to 375°.

Lightly oil a 9-inch pie pan or spray with a nonstick cooking spray.

In a large bowl, combine pears, apple juice, lemon juice, cinnamon, and brown sugar. Mix well. Spoon into prepared pan.

To prepare topping:

In another bowl, combine oats, flour, Grape Nuts®, cinnamon, and brown sugar. Mix well. Add oil and apple juice. Mix until all ingredients are moistened.

Sprinkle oat mixture evenly over pears.

Bake, uncovered, 35 minutes, until lightly browned.

Serve warm or cold.

Per serving:

167	Calories
3 g	Protein
4 g	Fat
32 g	Carbohydrate
25 mg	Sodium
0 mg	Cholesterol
4 g	Fiber

Cranberry Apple Crisp

The tartness of the cranberries mingled with the sweetness
of apples and honey makes this a truly unforgettable dessert.

Makes 8 servings

2   cups cranberries, fresh or frozen (if using frozen cranberries,
        measure and thaw before using)
2   medium, sweet apples, unpeeled, chopped into 1/2-inch pieces
        (2 cups)
1/4 cup sugar
1/4 cup water

Topping:
3/4 cup rolled oats
2   tablespoons whole wheat flour
1   teaspoon ground cinnamon
2   tablespoons firmly packed brown sugar
2   tablespoons vegetable oil
2   tablespoons apple juice

Preheat oven to 350°.
Lightly oil a 9-inch pie pan or spray with a nonstick cooking
spray.
In a medium saucepan, combine cranberries, apples, sugar, and
water. Cook over medium heat, stirring frequently, 5 to 10 minutes,
until cranberries pop. Remove from heat; spoon into prepared pan.

To prepare topping:
In a medium bowl, combine oats, flour, cinnamon, and brown
sugar, mixing well. Add oil and apple juice. Mix until all ingredients
are moistened. Distribute evenly over cranberry mixture.
Bake, uncovered, 30 minutes, until lightly browned.
Serve warm or cold.

Per serving:
      135 Calories
       2 g Protein
       4 g Fat
      24 g Carbohydrate
       2 mg Sodium
       0 mg Cholesterol
       2 g Fiber

Cool Orange Crisp

This no-bake crisp has a cool, delightful flavor. Make it when navel oranges are in season for a taste you won't forget.

Makes 6 servings

6   medium, sweet oranges, peeled and sectioned (3 cups)
             (discard white membrane)

Topping:
3/4   cup rolled oats
1/4   cup oat bran
1   tablespoon firmly-packed brown sugar
1/2   teaspoon ground cinnamon
2   teaspoons vegetable oil
2   tablespoons orange juice (unsweetened)

Glaze:
1   cup orange juice (unsweetened)
1   teaspoon grated fresh orange peel
1/4   cup honey
2   tablespoons cornstarch

Have an ungreased 9-inch pie pan ready.

Cut orange sections in half, crosswise, and place in a large bowl.

To prepare topping:

Preheat oven to 350°.

Lightly oil a 10 × 15-inch shallow baking pan or spray with a nonstick cooking spray.

In a small bowl, combine oats, oat bran, brown sugar, and cinnamon. Mix well. Add oil and orange juice. Mix until all ingredients are moistened. Spread in prepared pan.

Bake 10 to 12 minutes, until lightly browned. Stir several times while baking, breaking up any large lumps with the back of a spoon.

Cool in pan.

To prepare glaze:

In a small saucepan, combine all glaze ingredients. Bring to a boil over medium heat, stirring. Boil 2 minutes, stirring. Remove from heat. Pour glaze over oranges and toss gently.

To assemble:

Spoon oranges into pie pan. Sprinkle with oat topping.
Chill.
Spoon into dessert bowls or parfait glasses to serve.

Per serving:

191	Calories
4 g	Protein
3 g	Fat
41 g	Carbohydrate
2 mg	Sodium
0 mg	Cholesterol
4 g	Fiber

Strawberry Dessert Crisps

Prepare the topping and the sauce ahead of time and assemble these cool, refreshing crisps just before serving. They're a perfect summer dessert.

Makes 6 servings

6-1/2 cups sliced or quartered fresh strawberries

Topping:
3/4   cup rolled oats
1/4   cup oat bran
1   tablespoon firmly packed brown sugar
1/2   teaspoon ground cinnamon
2   teaspoons vegetable oil
2   tablespoons apple juice

Sauce:
1   cup plain nonfat yogurt
1/4   cup plus 2 tablespoons reduced-sugar or fruit-only strawberry
       jam
1   teaspoon sugar

To prepare topping:
Preheat oven to 350°.

Lightly oil a 10 × 15-inch shallow baking pan or spray with a nonstick cooking spray.

In a small bowl, combine oats, oat bran, brown sugar, and cinnamon. Mix well. Add oil and apple juice. Mix until all ingredients are moistened. Spread in prepared pan.

Bake 10 to 12 minutes, until lightly browned. Stir several times while baking, breaking up any large lumps with the back of a spoon.

Cool on pan and place in a covered jar or plastic bag until serving time.

To prepare sauce:
Combine all sauce ingredients in a small bowl. Mix well. Chill several hours or overnight.

At serving time:
Divide strawberries evenly into 6 serving bowls or tall-stemmed sherbet glasses. Spoon sauce over berries. Sprinkle with oat topping.

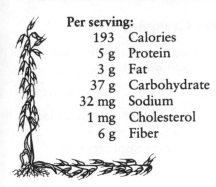

Per serving:

193	Calories
5 g	Protein
3 g	Fat
37 g	Carbohydrate
32 mg	Sodium
1 mg	Cholesterol
6 g	Fiber

Peach Melba Crispies

*Serve these delightful little fruit crisps warm with a scoop
of vanilla ice milk for a truly glorious dessert.*

Makes 6 servings

3   medium, ripe peaches, peeled, cut in half and pitted (canned,
         unsweetened peach halves may also be used)
2   tablespoons reduced-sugar or fruit-only raspberry jam

Topping:
3   tablespoons oat bran
3   tablespoons Grape Nuts® cereal
1   tablespoon firmly packed brown sugar
2   teaspoons vegetable oil
1   tablespoon water

Preheat oven to 375°.

Lightly oil a shallow baking pan or spray with a nonstick cooking spray.

Place peach halves, cut-side up, in prepared pan. (If necessary, slice a tiny sliver off the bottom of each one to keep it from rolling over.) Place 1 teaspoon of jam in the center of each half.

To prepare topping:

In a small bowl, combine oat bran, Grape Nuts®, and brown sugar. Mix well. Add oil and water. Mix until all ingredients are moistened. Place 1 tablespoon of topping on each peach half.

Bake 20 to 25 minutes, until lightly browned.

Serve warm or cold.

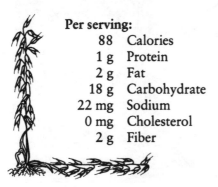

Per serving:
 88   Calories
 1 g Protein
 2 g Fat
 18 g Carbohydrate
 22 mg Sodium
 0 mg Cholesterol
 2 g Fiber

Cookies

Who doesn't love cookies? These tasty little morsels are traditionally baked for parties or holiday gatherings. However, when made with nutritious ingredients, cookies can be perfect snacks that will perk up an otherwise ordinary day.

Rolled oats and oat bran make excellent additions to cookies. The taste and texture are greatly enhanced by the addition of these high-fiber ingredients.

For drop cookies, rolled oats are a "natural". In place of the large amounts of butter in traditional dropped oatmeal cookies, I have used fruit juice or unsweetened applesauce. And, like the other baked goods in this book, many of the cookies are sweetened with honey, molasses, or pure maple syrup. This means that less oil can be used and the cookies will have the necessary amount of moist ingredients added. Also, as with the other sections, canola is my oil of choice. Although any vegetable oil will work in the recipes, and they all have about the same number of calories, many health professionals are recommending canola oil because it is low in saturated fat and high in monounsaturated fat, qualities that are believed to lower blood cholesterol levels.

I have found that an easy way to make rolled cookies is to form the dough into balls, cover them with wax paper, and flatten them using the bottom of a glass or a rolling pin. This method makes clean-up a lot easier, too.

Cookies bake best on a flat pan or one with very low sides. It's important, for uniform baking, to adjust the size of the pan so the amount of cookies fill the baking sheets completely. For small batches, use a small pan or invert a small baking pan and use the bottom. It is also best to bake cookies on the center oven rack and to not use two racks at the same time.

Because oven temperatures vary greatly, be sure to check cookies while they are baking. Bake them only until the bottoms are lightly browned. If you like crisper cookies, bake them a little longer or roll the dough a little thinner. As soon as cookies are done, they should be removed from the pan and cooled completely on a wire rack.

For added fiber and nutrition, replace one-fourth of the flour in your favorite rolled cookie recipes with oat bran, add rolled oats to your favorite drop cookies, and enjoy!

Orange Oatmeal Cookies

Warning: These cookies are habit-forming!

Makes 24 cookies

1-1/2	cups rolled oats
1/2	cup whole wheat flour
1	teaspoon baking powder
1/2	teaspoon ground cinnamon
3	tablespoons firmly packed brown sugar
1/4	cup chopped walnuts
1/2	cup raisins
1/2	cup frozen orange juice concentrate (unsweetened), thawed
1/2	cup water
2	tablespoons vegetable oil
1	teaspoon vanilla extract

In a large bowl, combine oats, flour, baking powder, cinnamon, and brown sugar. Mix well. Add walnuts and raisins.

In a small bowl, combine remaining ingredients, stirring with a spoon or wire whisk. Add to dry ingredients, mixing until all ingredients are moistened.

Let stand 15 minutes.

While mixture is standing, preheat oven to 375°.

Lightly oil a baking sheet or spray with a nonstick cooking spray.

Drop mixture by tablespoonfuls onto prepared baking sheet.

Bake 15 minutes, until bottoms of cookies are lightly browned.

Remove to a wire rack to cool.

Per cookie:

72	Calories
2 g	Protein
2 g	Fat
12 g	Carbohydrate
19 mg	Sodium
0 mg	Cholesterol
1 g	Fiber

Banana–Pecan Oatmeal Cookies

Banana lovers will flip over these moist, chewy morsels.
And, the riper the banana, the sweeter the cookies will be.

Makes 36 cookies

1	cup whole wheat flour
1	cup rolled oats
1/2	teaspoon baking soda
1/2	teaspoon ground cinnamon
1/4	teaspoon ground nutmeg
3	tablespoons chopped pecans
3	tablespoons vegetable oil
1/4	cup firmly packed brown sugar
1/2	cup mashed, ripe banana (1 medium banana)
1	teaspoon vanilla extract
1/4	cup water

Preheat oven to 375°.

Lightly oil a baking sheet or spray with a nonstick cooking spray.

In a large bowl, combine flour, oats, baking soda, spices and pecans. Mix well.

In a small bowl, combine remaining ingredients. Add to dry mixture. Mix until all ingredients are moistened.

Drop mixture by rounded teaspoonfuls onto prepared baking sheet.

Bake 10 to 12 minutes, until bottoms of cookies are lightly browned.

Remove to a wire rack to cool.

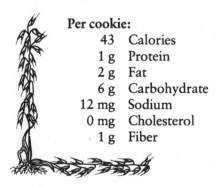

Per cookie:

43	Calories
1 g	Protein
2 g	Fat
6 g	Carbohydrate
12 mg	Sodium
0 mg	Cholesterol
1 g	Fiber

Peanut Oatmeal Cookies

Peanuts and raisins make these cookies very, very special.

Makes 28 cookies

1-1/2 cups rolled oats
1/2   cup whole wheat flour
1   teaspoon baking powder
1   teaspoon ground cinnamon
1/4   cup firmly packed brown sugar
1/4   cup chopped peanuts (unsalted)
1/4   cup raisins
1/2   cup applesauce (unsweetened)
1/2   cup apple juice
2   tablespoons vegetable oil
1   teaspoon vanilla extract

In a large bowl, combine oats, flour, baking powder, cinnamon, and brown sugar. Mix well.

Mix in peanuts and raisins.

In a small bowl, combine remaining ingredients. Add to oat mixture, mixing well.

Let stand 15 minutes.

While mixture is standing, preheat oven to 375°.

Lightly oil a baking sheet or spray with a nonstick cooking spray.

Stir batter once, then drop by level tablespoonfuls onto prepared baking sheet.

Bake 15 minutes, until bottoms of cookies are lightly browned.

Remove to a wire rack to cool.

Per cookie:
56	Calories
1 g	Protein
2 g	Fat
9 g	Carbohydrate
16 mg	Sodium
0 mg	Cholesterol
1 g	Fiber

Chinese Almond Cookies

These crispy treats taste just like the ones from our favorite Chinese restaurant.

Makes 24 cookies

1/2	cup whole wheat flour
1/4	cup all-purpose flour
1/4	cup oat bran
1	teaspoon baking powder
1/4	cup sugar
2	tablespoons vegetable oil
1/4	cup apple juice
1	teaspoon vanilla extract
1-1/4	teaspoons almond extract
24	almonds (unsalted)

Preheat oven to 375°.

Lightly oil a baking sheet or spray with a nonstick cooking spray.

In a medium bowl, combine both types of flour, oat bran, baking powder, and sugar. Mix well.

In a small bowl, combine oil, apple juice, and extracts. Add to dry ingredients and mix with a fork until ingredients are blended.

Work dough into a ball with your hands. Break off pieces of dough and roll into 24 balls, 1-1/4-inches in diameter. Wet your hands slightly as you work to keep dough from sticking. Place on prepared baking sheet, 1-1/2 inches apart. Place a sheet of wax paper over the cookies and flatten them to 1/4-inch thick, using a rolling pin or the bottom of a glass. Carefully remove wax paper.

Press an almond into the center of each cookie.

Bake 12 to 14 minutes, until bottoms of cookies are lightly browned.

Remove cookies to a wire rack to cool.

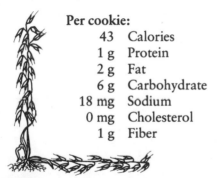

Per cookie:

43	Calories
1 g	Protein
2 g	Fat
6 g	Carbohydrate
18 mg	Sodium
0 mg	Cholesterol
1 g	Fiber

Ginger Snaps

Spiced just right, these delicious gems are crisp and tangy.

Makes 26 cookies

3/4	cup whole wheat flour
1/4	cup oat bran
1	teaspoon baking soda
1/2	teaspoon ground ginger
1/4	teaspoon ground cinnamon
1/8	teaspoon ground cloves
1/4	cup molasses
2	tablespoons vegetable oil
1	teaspoon vanilla extract
2	tablespoons water

Preheat oven to 375°.

Lightly oil a baking sheet or spray with a nonstick cooking spray.

In a large bowl, combine flour, oat bran, baking soda, and spices. Mix well.

In a small bowl, combine remaining ingredients. Add to dry mixture. Mix until ingredients are moistened.

Break off pieces of dough and roll into 26 one-inch balls. Wet your hands slightly as you work to keep dough from sticking. Place on prepared baking sheet, 1-1/2 inches apart. Place a sheet of wax paper over the cookies and flatten them to between 1/8- and 1/4-inch thick, using a rolling pin or the bottom of a glass. Carefully remove wax paper.

Bake 10 to 12 minutes, until bottoms of cookies are lightly browned.

Remove to a wire rack to cool.

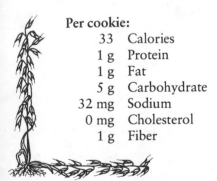

Per cookie:

33	Calories
1 g	Protein
1 g	Fat
5 g	Carbohydrate
32 mg	Sodium
0 mg	Cholesterol
1 g	Fiber

Lemon Sesame Cookies

Crisp and lemony, these cookies are sure to be a hit.

Makes 24 cookies

1/2	cup whole wheat flour
1/4	cup all-purpose flour
1/4	cup oat bran
1	teaspoon baking powder
1/4	cup sugar
2	tablespoons vegetable oil
1/4	cup orange juice (unsweetened)
1	teaspoon vanilla extract
1	teaspoon lemon extract
1	tablespoon sesame seeds

Preheat oven to 375°.

Lightly oil a baking sheet or spray with a nonstick cooking spray.

In a medium bowl, combine both types of flour, oat bran, baking powder, and sugar. Mix well.

In a small bowl, combine oil, orange juice, and extracts. Add to dry ingredients and mix until all ingredients are blended.

Work dough into a ball with your hands. Break off pieces of dough and roll into 24 balls, 1-1/4 inches in diameter. Wet your hands slightly as you work to keep dough from sticking. Place on prepared baking sheet, 1-1/2 inches apart. Place a sheet of wax paper over cookies and flatten them to 1/4-inch thick, using a rolling pin or the bottom of a glass. Carefully remove wax paper.

Sprinkle sesame seeds evenly over cookies. Press them gently into the cookies.

Bake 12 to 14 minutes, until bottoms of cookies are lightly browned.

Remove cookies to a wire rack to cool.

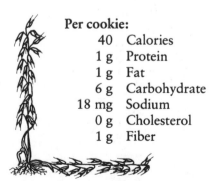

Per cookie:

40	Calories
1 g	Protein
1 g	Fat
6 g	Carbohydrate
18 mg	Sodium
0 g	Cholesterol
1 g	Fiber

Molasses Fruit 'n Nut Gems

These wonderful cookies are chock full of raisins and nuts.

Makes 36 cookies

1	cup whole wheat flour
1/2	cup oat bran
1-1/2	teaspoons baking soda
1/2	teaspoon ground cinnamon
1/4	teaspoon ground nutmeg
1/16	teaspoon ground allspice
1/16	teaspoon ground cloves
3	tablespoons chopped walnuts
1/3	cup raisins
3	tablespoons vegetable oil
1/4	cup plus 2 tablespoons molasses
3	tablespoons orange juice (unsweetened)
1	teaspoon vanilla extract

Preheat oven to 375°.

Lightly oil a baking sheet or spray with a nonstick cooking spray.

In a large bowl, combine flour, oat bran, baking soda, and spices. Mix well. Add walnuts and raisins.

In a small bowl, combine remaining ingredients. Add to dry mixture, mixing until ingredients are moistened.

Break off pieces of dough and roll into 36 balls, 1-1/4 inches in diameter. Wet your hands slightly as you work to keep dough from sticking. Place on prepared baking sheet. Place a sheet of wax paper over cookies and flatten them to 1/4-inch thick, using a rolling pin or the bottom of a glass. Carefully remove wax paper.

Bake 10 to 12 minutes, until bottoms of cookies are lightly browned. Remove to a wire rack to cool.

Per cookie:

43	Calories
1 g	Protein
2 g	Fat
7 g	Carbohydrate
35 mg	Sodium
0 mg	Cholesterol
1 g	Fiber

Cinnamon Oat Crisps

These delicate, crisp treats are great to serve alongside your favorite fruit dessert. They also make a delicious snack.

Makes 45 cookies

1	cup whole wheat flour
1/2	cup rolled oats
1	teaspoon baking powder
3	tablespoons sugar
3	tablespoons vegetable oil
1/4	cup plus 2 teaspoons apple juice

Topping:

1	tablespoon sugar
1	teaspoon ground cinnamon

Preheat oven to 375°.

Have an ungreased baking sheet ready.

In a large bowl, combine flour, oats, baking powder, and sugar. Mix well.

Add oil. Mix with a fork or pastry blender until oil is evenly distributed and mixture is crumbly.

Add apple juice. Mix until all ingredients are moistened.

With your hands, shape dough into a ball. Place on a lightly floured surface. Place a sheet of wax paper over the dough and roll to 1/8-inch thick. Carefully remove wax paper.

Combine sugar and cinnamon and sprinkle evenly over dough. Cut into 2-inch squares. Using a spatula, carefully place cookies on baking sheet.

Bake 8 minutes, until bottoms of cookies are lightly browned.

Remove cookies to a wire rack to cool.

Per cookie:

26	Calories
1 g	Protein
1 g	Fat
4 g	Carbohydrate
10 mg	Sodium
0 mg	Cholesterol
1 g	Fiber

Cocoa Specials

A hint of coconut gives these tasty cookies a special twist.

Makes 26 cookies

1/3	cup oat bran
2/3	cup rolled oats
3	tablespoons whole wheat flour
1	teaspoon baking powder
1/3	cup firmly packed brown sugar
3	tablespoons cocoa (unsweetened)
2	tablespoons nonfat dry milk
3	tablespoons vegetable oil
3	tablespoons water
1	teaspoon vanilla extract
1/2	teaspoon coconut extract

Preheat oven to 375°.

Lightly oil a baking sheet or spray with a nonstick cooking spray.

In a large bowl, combine dry ingredients. Mix well, breaking up any lumps of brown sugar.

In a small bowl, combine remaining ingredients. Add to dry mixture, mixing until all ingredients are moistened.

Break off pieces of dough and roll into 26 one-inch balls. Wet your hands slightly as you work to keep dough from sticking. Place on prepared baking sheet, 2 inches apart. Place a piece of wax paper over the cookies and flatten them to 1/4-inch thick, using a rolling pin or the bottom of a glass. Carefully remove wax paper.

Bake 10 to 12 minutes until bottoms of cookies are lightly browned.

Remove to a wire rack to cool.

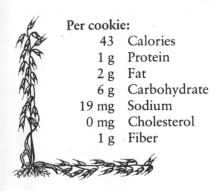

Per cookie:	
43	Calories
1 g	Protein
2 g	Fat
6 g	Carbohydrate
19 mg	Sodium
0 mg	Cholesterol
1 g	Fiber

Fig Bars

You'll love the moist fig filling inside the flaky oat crust of these tender-sweet cookies.

Makes 24 bars

Filling:

8   ounces dried figs, cut in half
1   teaspoon grated fresh orange peel
1/2   cup apple juice
2   tablespoons oat bran

Crust:

3/4   cup all-purpose flour
1   cup whole wheat flour
1/4   cup oat bran
1/4   cup sugar
1/4   cup vegetable oil
1/2   cup plus 2 tablespoons water

Preheat oven to 350°.
Lightly oil a baking sheet or spray with a nonstick cooking spray.

To prepare filling:

In a blender container, combine figs, orange peel, and apple juice. Blend until figs are in the form of a thick puree. Place in a small bowl and stir in oat bran. Set aside.

To prepare crust:

In a medium bowl, combine both types of flour, oat bran, and sugar. Mix well. Add oil and water. Mix with a fork, and then with your hands, until mixture holds together in a ball.

Shape dough into a log and place on a lightly floured surface. Roll into a 12 × 14-inch rectangle. Cut the rectangle lengthwise into 3 strips.

To assemble:

Spoon filling down the center of each strip. Fold over and seal the edges by crimping with a fork. Place rolls on prepared baking sheet. Flatten them slightly with your hand.

Bake 20 minutes.

Remove to a wire rack to cool. When cool, cut each log into 1-1/2 inch bars.

Per bar:

91	Calories
2 g	Protein
3 g	Fat
16 g	Carbohydrate
1 mg	Sodium
0 mg	Cholesterol
2 g	Fiber

Brown Sugar Crisps

So crisp and delicious, with the taste of brown sugar and
vanilla, these cookies are great for snacking.

Makes 30 cookies

1/2   cup plus 2 tablespoons whole wheat flour
1/4   cup all-purpose flour
1/4   cup oat bran
1   teaspoon baking powder
1/4   cup firmly packed brown sugar
2   tablespoons vegetable oil
1-1/2 teaspoons vanilla extract
1/4   cup water

Preheat oven to 375°.

Lightly oil a baking sheet or spray with a nonstick cooking spray.

In a medium bowl, combine both types of flour, oat bran, and baking powder. Mix well.

In a small bowl, combine remaining ingredients. Mix well. Add to dry mixture, mixing until all ingredients are moistened.

Break off pieces of dough and roll into 30 one-inch balls. Wet your hands slightly as you work to keep dough from sticking. Place 2 inches apart on prepared baking sheet. Place a piece of wax paper over cookies and flatten them to between 1/8- and 1/4-inch thick, using a rolling pin or the bottom of a glass. Carefully remove wax paper.

Bake 10 to 12 minutes until edges and bottoms of cookies are lightly browned.

Remove to a wire rack to cool.

Per cookie:
31	Calories
1 g	Protein
1 g	Fat
5 g	Carbohydrate
15 mg	Sodium
0 mg	Cholesterol
1 g	Fiber

Jam-Filled Cookies

Use any flavor of jam in these festive-looking cookies, or make them with several different flavors for a really colorful platter.

Makes 24 cookies

3/4	cup whole wheat flour
1/4	cup oat bran
1	teaspoon baking powder
1/4	cup sugar
2	tablespoons vegetable oil
1/4	cup apple juice
1-1/2	teaspoons vanilla extract
	Few drops lemon *or* orange extract
2	tablespoons reduced-sugar or fruit-only jam, any flavor

Preheat oven to 375°.

Lightly oil a baking sheet or spray with a nonstick cooking spray.

In a large bowl, combine flour, oat bran, baking powder, and sugar. Mix well.

In a small bowl, combine remaining ingredients, *except* jam. Add to dry ingredients and mix until all ingredients are moistened.

Break off pieces of dough and roll into 24 balls, 1-1/4-inches in diameter. Wet your hands slightly as you work to keep dough from sticking. Place on prepared baking sheet, 1-1/2 inches apart. Place a sheet of wax paper over the cookies and flatten them to 1/4-inch thick, using a rolling pin or the bottom of a glass. Carefully remove wax paper.

Using the back of a 1/4-teaspoon measuring spoon, make an indentation in the center of each cookie. Wet the spoon very slightly to keep it from sticking to the dough.

Place 1/4 teaspoon of jam in each indentation.

Bake 12 to 14 minutes, until bottoms of cookies are lightly browned. Remove to a wire rack to cool.

Per cookie:

40	Calories
1 g	Protein
1 g	Fat
7 g	Carbohydrate
18 mg	Sodium
0 mg	Cholesterol
1 g	Fiber

Lemon Bars

*Everyone who tastes these lemony confections falls in
love with them.*

Makes 16 bars

Crust:

2	tablespoons oat bran
2/3	cup rolled oats
3	tablespoons graham cracker crumbs
2	tablespoons sugar
2	tablespoons whole wheat flour
3	tablespoons vegetable oil
1/4	cup skim milk
1/4	teaspoon lemon extract

Topping:

1	egg white
1/3	cup sugar
1/2	teaspoon lemon extract
1	teaspoon grated fresh lemon peel

Preheat oven to 350°.

Lightly oil an 8-inch square baking pan or spray with a nonstick cooking spray.

To prepare crust:

In a large bowl, combine oat bran, rolled oats, graham cracker crumbs, sugar, and flour. Mix well.

In a small bowl, combine oil, milk, and lemon extract. Add to dry mixture, mixing until all ingredients are moistened. Spread mixture evenly in prepared pan.

Bake 15 minutes.

To prepare topping:

While crust is baking, combine topping ingredients in a small bowl. Beat with a fork or wire whisk until blended. Spread evenly over hot crust.

Return to oven and bake 18 minutes more. (Any large bubbles that form during baking will deflate as bars cool.)

Cool in pan 10 minutes, then cut into 16 squares and remove to a wire rack to finish cooling.

Per bar:

- 72 Calories
- 1 g Protein
- 3 g Fat
- 10 g Carbohydrate
- 14 mg Sodium
- 0 mg Cholesterol
- 1 g Fiber

Apricot–Raisin Oat Bars

These bars are either "cake-like cookies" or "cookie-like cakes". Whichever the case, they're delicious.

Makes 16 bars

1/2	cup water
1/3	cup pure maple syrup
1/2	cup raisins
1/2	cup chopped, dried apricots*
3/4	cup whole wheat flour
3/4	cup rolled oats
1/2	teaspoon baking soda
1	teaspoon ground cinnamon
2	tablespoons vegetable oil

In a small saucepan, combine water, 1 tablespoon of the maple syrup, raisins, and apricots. Bring to a boil over medium heat. Reduce heat to low and simmer 10 minutes. Remove from heat.

Preheat oven to 350°.

Lightly oil an 8-inch square baking pan or spray with a nonstick cooking spray.

In a large bowl, combine flour, oats, baking soda, and cinnamon. Mix well. Add oil and remaining maple syrup, along with apricot mixture. Mix until well blended.

Place in prepared pan. Press mixture firmly into place, wetting your fingertips slightly to prevent sticking.

Bake 25 minutes, until a toothpick inserted in the center comes out clean.

Cool in pan on a wire rack.

Cut into 16 squares to serve.

*An easy way to chop dried fruit is to snip it with kitchen shears.

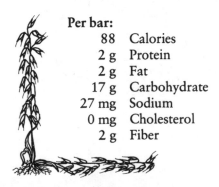

Per bar:

88	Calories
2 g	Protein
2 g	Fat
17 g	Carbohydrate
27 mg	Sodium
0 mg	Cholesterol
2 g	Fiber

Chocolate–Almond Oat Bars

These rich cookie bars are sure to satisfy anyone's sweet tooth.

Makes 16 bars

Crust:

1/3	cup oat bran
2/3	cup rolled oats
3	tablespoons firmly packed brown sugar
2	tablespoons nonfat dry milk
2	tablespoons whole wheat flour
3	tablespoons vegetable oil
1/4	cup apple juice

Topping:

2	tablespoons oat bran
2	tablespoons wheat germ
3	tablespoons cocoa (unsweetened)
1/4	cup honey
1-1/2	teaspoons almond extract

Preheat oven to 350°.

Lightly oil an 8-inch square baking pan or spray with a nonstick cooking spray.

To prepare crust:

In a large bowl, combine oat bran, rolled oats, brown sugar, dry milk, and flour. Mix well. Add oil and apple juice, mixing until all ingredients are moistened. Pat mixture evenly in prepared pan, wetting your fingers slightly to prevent sticking. Bake 15 minutes.

To prepare topping:

While crust is baking, combine topping ingredients in a small bowl. Mix well. Spread evenly over hot crust, using a table knife.

Return to oven and bake 15 minutes more.

Cool in pan 10 minutes, then cut into 16 squares and remove to a wire rack to finish cooling.

Per bar:

85	Calories
2 g	Protein
3 g	Fat
13 g	Carbohydrate
4 mg	Sodium
0 mg	Cholesterol
1 g	Fiber

Almond Granola Bars

These taste-tempting, almond-flavored bars make a
wonderful snack or lunchbox treat.

Makes 16 bars

1-1/2   cups rolled oats
1/4   cup oat bran
1/4   cup finely chopped almonds
1/2   teaspoon ground cinnamon
2   tablespoons plus 1 teaspoon vegetable oil
1/3   cup honey
1/2   teaspoon vanilla extract
3/4   teaspoon almond extract

Preheat oven to 350°.

Lightly oil a baking sheet or spray with a nonstick cooking spray.

In a large bowl, combine oats, oat bran, almonds, and cinnamon. Mix well.

In a small bowl, combine remaining ingredients. Add to dry mixture, mixing until all ingredients are moistened.

Place mixture on prepared sheet and press into the shape of a rectangle that measures 7 inches wide, 9 inches long, and 1/2 inch high. Wet your hands slightly as you work and press mixture firmly into place.

Bake 12 minutes. Remove from oven and cut into 16 bars, using a very sharp knife. (Use a cutting, rather than a sawing motion.) Separate bars slightly and return to oven for 3 to 5 minutes more. The browner the bottoms of the bars, the crisper they will be when cool. (It is normal for the edges of the bars to crumble slightly when cut. Eat the crumbs as an immediate snack!)

Remove to a wire rack to cool.

Per bar:

86	Calories
2 g	Protein
4 g	Fat
12 g	Carbohydrate
1 mg	Sodium
0 mg	Cholesterol
1 g	Fiber

Potpourri

This is a miscellaneous section that contains everything from pâtés and spreads through fruitshakes and crackers. There are so many places where the wonderful, tasty high fiber of oats can be incorporated into everyday dishes.

The following pages will give you recipes for adding oats to foods in the following ways:

- In a blender, combine oat bran with fruit and skim milk for a really high-fiber fruitshake.
- Substitute oat bran for part of the flour in cracker recipes.
- Make biscuits and rolls, using oat bran in place of part of the flour.
- Put rolled oats and dried fruit in a food processor and roll into chewy, candy-like confections.
- Toast rolled oats and use them as a coating for frozen bananas.
- Use oat bran as a thickener for pâtés and spreads.
- Soak steel-cut oats in hot water and add to breads for a unique crunch.
- Make delicious cornsticks by substituting oat bran for part of the cornmeal.

Oat Bran Rusks

Similar to mandelbrot or zwieback, these small slices of bread are toasted to make them crisp. They're an ideal snack to have with a cup of hot tea or coffee.

Makes 20 rusks

1	cup whole wheat flour
1/2	cup all-purpose flour
1/2	cup oat bran
2	teaspoons baking powder
2	egg whites
1/3	cup sugar
3	tablespoons vegetable oil
1/4	cup orange juice (unsweetened)
1	teaspoon vanilla extract
1	teaspoon almond extract

Preheat oven to 350°.

Lightly oil a baking sheet or spray with a nonstick cooking spray.

In a large bowl, combine both types of flour, oat bran, and baking powder. Mix well.

In a small bowl, combine remaining ingredients. Beat with a fork or wire whisk until blended. Add to dry mixture, mixing until all ingredients are moistened. With your hands, shape dough into a log. Place on prepared baking sheet and pat dough into a flat loaf that measures 3 inches wide, 12 inches long, and 1 inch high.

Bake 30 minutes, until bottom of loaf is lightly browned.

Remove pan from oven, but do not turn off oven. With a sharp knife, carefully slice hot loaf into 1/2-inch slices. (A serrated knife works best.) Lay slices down flat on pan and return to oven. Turn oven off and let rusks stay inside to toast until oven is cool.

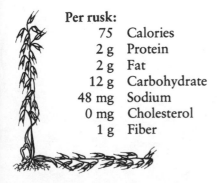

Per rusk:

75	Calories
2 g	Protein
2 g	Fat
12 g	Carbohydrate
48 mg	Sodium
0 mg	Cholesterol
1 g	Fiber

English Tea Biscuits

Sweeter than crackers, but not as sweet as cookies, these crunchy treats are perfect for snacks.

Makes 30 biscuits

1/2	cup oat flour
3/4	cup whole wheat flour
1/4	cup oat bran
1/2	teaspoon baking powder
1	egg white
3	tablespoons vegetable oil
1/4	cup firmly packed brown sugar
3	tablespoons water

Preheat oven to 375°.

Lightly oil a baking sheet or spray with a nonstick cooking spray.

In a large bowl, combine both types of flour, oat bran, and baking powder. Mix well.

In a small bowl, combine remaining ingredients. Beat with a fork or wire whisk until blended. Add to dry mixture, mixing until all ingredients are blended.

Work dough into a ball with your hands. Place on a lightly floured surface. Place a sheet of wax paper over the dough and roll to between 1/8- and 1/4-inch thick. Carefully remove wax paper.

Using a sharp knife, cut dough into 2-inch squares. Place on prepared baking sheet. Prick each biscuit 2 or 3 times with a fork.

Bake 10 to 12 minutes, until bottoms of biscuits are lightly browned.* Remove to a rack to cool.

*The thinner you roll the dough, the crisper the biscuits will be and the shorter the baking time.

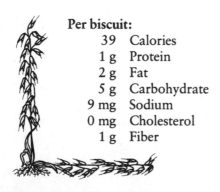

Per biscuit:

39	Calories
1 g	Protein
2 g	Fat
5 g	Carbohydrate
9 mg	Sodium
0 mg	Cholesterol
1 g	Fiber

Oat 'n Chive Snackers

These crunchy, herbed crackers make delicious, snacks.

Makes 42 crackers

1/2	cup rolled oats
1/4	cup oat bran
1/2	cup whole wheat flour
1/4	cup all-purpose flour
1	teaspoon baking powder
2	teaspoons sugar
1/2	teaspoon salt
1	tablespoon dried chives
3	tablespoons vegetable oil
1/4	cup plus 3 tablespoons water
	Salt for topping (optional)

Preheat oven to 400°.

Have an ungreased baking sheet ready.

In a large bowl, combine oats, oat bran, both types of flour, baking powder, sugar, salt, and chives. Mix well.

Add oil. Mix with a fork or pastry blender until oil is evenly distributed and mixture is crumbly.

Add water. Mix until all ingredients are moistened.

With your hands, shape dough into a ball. Divide dough in half and, working with half at a time, place on a lightly floured surface. Place a piece of wax paper over the dough and roll to 1/8-inch thick. Carefully remove wax paper.

Using a sharp knife, cut dough into 2-inch squares. Place on baking sheet. Prick each cracker several times with a fork. Sprinkle lightly with salt, if desired.

Bake 10 to 12 minutes, until edges and bottoms of crackers are lightly browned. Remove crackers to a wire rack to cool.

Per cracker:

23	Calories
1 g	Protein
1 g	Fat
3 g	Carbohydrate
36 mg	Sodium
0 mg	Cholesterol
1 g	Fiber

Garlic Oat Crackers

These crisp crackers are perfect as snacks, either alone or with your favorite topping.

Makes 52 crackers

1-1/2 cups rolled oats
1/4   cup whole wheat flour
1/4   cup all-purpose flour
1/3   cup wheat germ
2   teaspoons sugar
1/4   teaspoon garlic powder
1/4   teaspoon salt
1/4   cup vegetable oil
1/2   cup water
      Sesame seeds or poppy seeds (optional)

Preheat oven to 375°.

Have two ungreased baking sheets ready.

Place oats in a blender container and blend until they are ground into flour. Place in a medium bowl. Add remaining dry ingredients. Mix well.

Add oil. Mix with a fork until mixture is in the form of coarse crumbs. Add water, mixing until all ingredients are moistened.

Break off pieces of dough and roll into 52 balls, 3/4-inch in diameter. Place on baking sheet. Place a piece of wax paper over the crackers and flatten them to 1/8-inch thick, using a rolling pin or the bottom of a glass. Carefully remove wax paper.

If desired, sprinkle sesame seeds or poppy seeds over crackers and press them in gently.

Bake 15 to 17 minutes, until bottoms of crackers are lightly browned.

Remove to a wire rack to cool.

Per cracker:
    26   Calories
   1 g   Protein
   1 g   Fat
   3 g   Carbohydrate
 11 mg   Sodium
  0 mg   Cholesterol
   1 g   Fiber

Garlic Sticks

*When you feel like "munching", these crunchy
breadsticks will really hit the spot. They're also great with
your favorite soup or salad.*

Makes 50 breadsticks

3/4   cup whole wheat flour
1/4   cup all-purpose flour
1/2   cup oat bran
1/2   cup wheat germ
1/2   teaspoon baking powder
2/3   cup skim milk
2   tablespoons vegetable oil
2   teaspoons honey
        Salt to taste
        Garlic powder to taste

Preheat oven to 350°.

Have two ungreased baking sheets ready.

In a large bowl, combine dry ingredients. Mix well.

In a small bowl, whisk together remaining ingredients. Add to dry mixture, mixing until all ingredients are moistened.

With your hands, shape dough into a ball. Place on a lightly floured surface. Place a sheet of wax paper over the dough and roll into a 9 × 15-inch rectangle, 1/4-inch thick. (For crisper sticks, roll dough thinner.) Carefully remove wax paper.

Sprinkle dough lightly with salt and garlic powder. Cut dough in half lengthwise, then into 50 sticks 1/2-inch wide. Using a spatula, carefully place strips on baking sheet.

Bake 20 to 25 minutes, until bottoms of breadsticks are lightly browned. (Thinner breadsticks will take less time to bake.)

Remove to a rack to cool.

Per breadstick:
          23 Calories
          1 g Protein
          1 g Fat
          3 g Carbohydrate
        6 mg Sodium
        0 mg Cholesterol
          1 g Fiber

Corn Sticks

Served hot, right from the oven, these crisp oat bran and cornsticks will definitely bring rave reviews.

Makes 14 sticks

1/2	cup whole wheat flour
1/2	cup oat bran
1	cup yellow cornmeal
2	tablespoons sugar
1	tablespoon baking powder
1/8	teaspoon salt
1	cup skim milk
1	tablespoon lemon juice
2	egg whites
3	tablespoons vegetable oil

Preheat oven to 425°.

Lightly oil 2 cornstick pans or spray with a nonstick cooking spray.

Place oiled pans in the oven to preheat while preparing the batter.

In a large bowl, combine flour, oat bran, cornmeal, sugar, baking powder, and salt. Mix well.

In a small bowl, combine milk and lemon juice. Let stand 1 minute. Add egg whites and oil. Beat with a fork or wire whisk until blended. Add to dry mixture, mixing just until all ingredients are moistened.

Spoon batter into hot pans.

Bake 15 minutes, until golden.

Remove from pan onto a wire rack. Serve hot for best flavor and texture.

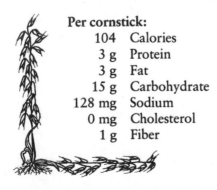

Per cornstick:

104	Calories
3 g	Protein
3 g	Fat
15 g	Carbohydrate
128 mg	Sodium
0 mg	Cholesterol
1 g	Fiber

Steel-Cut Scones

The steel-cut oats in this English favorite give a chewy texture and a bit of crunch to a wonderful, "go-with-anything" bread. Serve them warm, right from the oven, or pop them in the toaster to reheat. Toasting makes the bits of oats even crunchier.

Makes 8 scones

1/2	cup steel-cut oats
1/4	cup nonfat dry milk
1/2	cup boiling water
1	tablespoon vegetable oil
1/2	cup all-purpose flour
1/4	cup whole wheat flour
1-1/2	teaspoons baking powder
1	tablespoon sugar

In a small bowl, combine oats and dry milk. Add boiling water and oil and let mixture cool to room temperature.

Preheat oven to 375°.

Lightly oil a 10-inch cast iron skillet or spray with a nonstick cooking spray.

In a medium bowl, combine remaining ingredients, mixing well. Add oat mixture. Mix until all ingredients are moistened. Form dough into a ball.

Press dough into the bottom of prepared skillet. Wet hands slightly, if necessary, to prevent sticking. With a sharp knife, cut the dough into 8 pie-shaped wedges.

Bake 18 minutes, until bottoms of scones are lightly browned.

Remove to a rack.

Serve warm for best flavor and texture.

Per scone:

112	Calories
4 g	Protein
3 g	Fat
19 g	Carbohydrate
92 mg	Sodium
0 mg	Cholesterol
2 g	Fiber

Beer 'n Rye Rolls

These chewy, crusty rolls are easily made in a muffin pan.
You'll love them plain or with your favorite sandwich
filling.

Makes 8 rolls

1/2	cup whole wheat flour
1/2	cup all-purpose flour
1/2	cup rye flour
3/4	cup oat bran
2-1/2	teaspoons baking powder
1/4	teaspoon salt
2	tablespoons sugar
1/8	teaspoon garlic powder
1-1/2	teaspoons caraway seeds
1	12-ounce can light beer (1-1/2 cups), at room temperature

Preheat oven to 375°.

Lightly oil 8 muffins cups or spray with a nonstick cooking spray.

In a large bowl, combine all ingredients, *except* beer. Mix well.

Add beer, stirring until foam subsides and all ingredients are moistened.

Divide mixture into prepared muffin cups.

Bake 20 to 22 minutes, until firm and lightly browned. Remove rolls to a rack to cool.

Serve warm for best flavor.

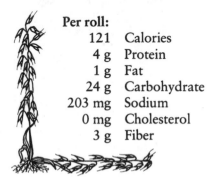

Per roll:

121	Calories
4 g	Protein
1 g	Fat
24 g	Carbohydrate
203 mg	Sodium
0 mg	Cholesterol
3 g	Fiber

Oat Bran Biscuits

Oat bran gives these flaky biscuits a toasty, "oaty" flavor.
Try them alongside any entrée or use them for a change-
of-pace sandwich.

Makes 10 biscuits

1	cup all-purpose flour
3/4	cup whole wheat flour
1/4	cup oat bran
1	tablespoon plus 1 teaspoon baking powder
1/4	teaspoon salt
4	tablespoons vegetable oil
3/4	cup skim milk

Preheat oven to 450°.

Lightly oil a baking sheet or spray with a nonstick cooking spray.

In a large bowl, combine both types of flour, oat bran, baking powder, and salt. Mix well.

Add oil. Mix with a fork or pastry blender until mixture resembles coarse crumbs.

Add milk. Stir until dry ingredients are moistened.

Place dough on a floured surface and knead a few times until dough holds together in a ball. Place a sheet of wax paper over dough and roll to 1/4-inch thick. Carefully remove wax paper and fold dough in half, making it now 1/2-inch thick. Using a 3-inch biscuit cutter or a glass, cut 10 biscuits. (Scraps can be put together and rolled again.)

Place on prepared baking sheet.

Bake 10 minutes, until bottoms of biscuits are lightly browned.

Remove to a wire rack to cool.

Serve warm for best flavor.

Per biscuit:

139	Calories
4 g	Protein
6 g	Fat
18 g	Carbohydrate
234 mg	Sodium
0 mg	Cholesterol
2 g	Fiber

Herbed Bread Twists

Almost a breadstick, almost a roll, what could go better with a bowl of soup than these crusty, herbed twists? (Be sure to read about yeast breads on page 153.)

Makes 32 twists

3/4   cup whole wheat flour
3/4   cup all-purpose flour
3/4   cup oat bran
1   tablespoon dried chives
2   teaspoons dried parsley flakes
1   teaspoon caraway seeds
1   cup lukewarm water (105° to 115°)
1   tablespoon honey
1   package active dry yeast
2   tablespoons vegetable oil
       Salt to taste

Lightly oil a baking sheet or spray with a nonstick cooking spray.

In a large bowl, combine both types of flour, oat bran, chives, parsley, and caraway seeds.

Stir 1 teaspoon of the honey into the lukewarm water in a small bowl. Sprinkle with the yeast. Let stand 5 minutes.

Stir remaining honey and oil into yeast mixture. Add to flour, mixing with a wooden spoon and then with your hands until all of the flour is incorporated into the dough.

Place dough in a large oiled bowl and brush the top of the dough lightly with oil. (Both the bowl and the dough can be sprayed with a nonstick cooking spray if you prefer.) Cover the bowl with a damp towel and put in a warm place for 1 hour to rise.

Punch the dough down and then turn it out onto a floured surface. (Use all-purpose flour.) Knead it about 10 times.

Divide the dough into 4 equal parts. One at a time, roll each piece into a 10-inch square, adding more flour to the surface as necessary to keep dough from sticking. Cut each square into 4 equal strips. Then cut each strip in half, crosswise. Twist each piece so that it resembles a twisted rope.

Place twists on prepared baking sheet, about 2 inches apart. Sprinkle lightly with salt.

Cover with a dry towel and put in a warm place to rise once more, for 30 minutes.

Preheat oven to 400°.

Bake 15 minutes, until bottoms of twists are lightly browned.

Remove to a wire rack to cool.

Serve warm for best flavor and texture. To reheat, place twists directly on the rack of a preheated oven or toaster oven at 350° for 5 minutes.

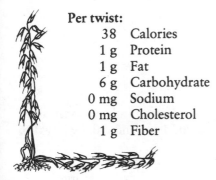

Per twist:

38	Calories
1 g	Protein
1 g	Fat
6 g	Carbohydrate
0 mg	Sodium
0 mg	Cholesterol
1 g	Fiber

Pastry Pie Crust

This easy pastry crust is perfect for fruit pies and pumpkin pies and can also be prebaked for no-bake fillings such as strawberries and gelatin mixtures.

Makes one 9-inch crust (8 servings)

2/3	cup rolled oats
1/2	cup whole wheat flour
1/2	teaspoon baking powder
1/4	cup plus 1 tablespoon cold milk
3	tablespoons vegetable oil

Have a 9-inch pie pan ready.

Place oats in a blender container and blend until the consistency of flour. Place in a medium bowl and add flour and baking powder. Mix well.

With a fork, stir in milk and oil. Work dough into a ball, using your hands. Roll dough between 2 sheets of wax paper into a 12-inch circle. Carefully remove top sheet of wax paper and invert crust into pie pan. Fit crust into pan, leaving an overhang. Carefully remove remaining wax paper. Bend edges of crust under and flute dough with your fingers or with a fork.

For baked fillings, fill crust and bake according to directions.

For no-bake fillings, prick the bottom and sides of crust about 40 times with a fork. Bake crust in a preheated 450° oven for 10 minutes. Cool completely on a wire rack before filling.

Per serving:

102	Calories
2 g	Protein
6 g	Fat
10 g	Carbohydrate
32 mg	Sodium
1 mg	Cholesterol
2 g	Fiber

Triple Crown Pie Crust

The winning combination of graham cracker crumbs, wheat germ, and oat bran gave this unusual crust its name.

Makes one 9-inch crust (8 servings)

1/3	cup oat bran
1/4	cup graham cracker crumbs
1/4	cup wheat germ
1	tablespoon sugar
1/4	teaspoon ground cinnamon
1/4	cup margarine, melted

Preheat oven to 350°.

Very lightly oil a 9-inch pie pan or spray with a nonstick cooking spray.

In a small bowl, combine all crust ingredients, *except* margarine. Mix well. Place in prepared pie pan. Add margarine. Mix until all ingredients are moistened. Press crumbs firmly into bottom of pan and along the sides, forming a crust.

Bake 10 minutes.

Crust can be filled with no-bake fillings or with those that require further baking.

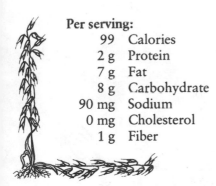

Per serving:

99	Calories
2 g	Protein
7 g	Fat
8 g	Carbohydrate
90 mg	Sodium
0 mg	Cholesterol
1 g	Fiber

Hummus Spread

Although many cookbooks have a recipe for this Middle East favorite, most of them contain a lot of oil. This one not only has no oil but also has oat bran added to make it high in fiber and very spreadable. It makes a great sandwich—especially in a whole wheat pita.

Makes 4 servings (enough for 4 sandwiches)

1	1-pound can chick peas (garbanzo beans), rinsed and drained
1	tablespoon lemon juice
1/4	teaspoon salt
2	cloves garlic, minced
1/4	cup water
1/4	cup oat bran

In a blender container, combine all ingredients, *except* oat bran. Blend until smooth. Spoon into a bowl and add oat bran. Mix well.
Cover and chill.
Serve cold as a sandwich filling or as a spread for crackers.

Per serving:
159	Calories
7 g	Protein
2 g	Fat
29 g	Carbohydrate
476 mg	Sodium
0 mg	Cholesterol
3 g	Fiber

Mushroom Pâté

A delicious combination of subtle flavors, this pâté makes a great spread for toast or crackers.

Makes 6 servings

2	tablespoons olive oil
1/2	pound mushrooms, sliced
1/2	cup chopped onions
1	clove garlic, minced
1/8	teaspoon salt
1/8	teaspoon pepper
1/8	teaspoon dried oregano
1/8	teaspoon dried basil
2	tablespoons skim milk
1/4	cup oat bran
2	tablespoons wheat germ

Heat oil in a large nonstick skillet over medium heat. Add mushrooms, onions, garlic, and spices. Cook 10 to 15 minutes, until mushrooms and onions are lightly browned and most of the liquid has cooked out. Stir occasionally while cooking.

Place mushroom mixture in a blender container and add milk. Blend until mushrooms are finely chopped. Do not overblend. Spoon into a bowl and add oat bran and wheat germ. Mix well. (For a thicker consistency, add more oat bran.)

Line a small bowl with plastic wrap. Spoon pâté into bowl, cover, and chill several hours or overnight.

To serve, invert onto a serving plate and remove plastic wrap. Serve cold.

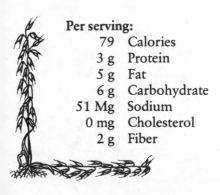

Per serving:

79	Calories
3 g	Protein
5 g	Fat
6 g	Carbohydrate
51 Mg	Sodium
0 mg	Cholesterol
2 g	Fiber

Strawberry Smoothie

Frozen berries make this shake so thick, you can almost eat it with a spoon.

Makes 2 servings

2   tablespoons oat bran
3   tablespoons nonfat dry milk
1   cup water
1   tablespoon sugar or honey
2   cups frozen strawberries (unsweetened), still frozen

In a blender container, combine oat bran and dry milk; blend to a powder. Add remaining ingredients, *except* strawberries. Turn on blender and carefully add berries while blending. Blend on high until berries are pureed and mixture is smooth.

Serve right away.

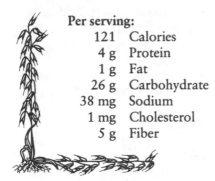

Per serving:
121   Calories
4 g   Protein
1 g   Fat
26 g   Carbohydrate
38 mg Sodium
1 mg   Cholesterol
5 g   Fiber

Tropical Treat

Oat bran adds fiber to this quick, delicious drink that's as cool as a tropical breeze.

Makes 2 servings

2	tablespoons oat bran
3	tablespoons nonfat dry milk
1/2	small ripe banana
1/4	cup canned crushed pineapple (unsweetened), undrained
1/2	cup frozen strawberries (unsweetened), still frozen
1/2	cup orange juice (unsweetened)
1/4	cup water
2	teaspoons sugar or honey
1/8	teaspoon coconut extract
1/2	cup ice cubes (5 small cubes)

In a blender container, combine oat bran and dry milk. Blend to a powder. Add remaining ingredients, *except* ice. Blend until smooth.

Add ice while blending. Blend on high until ice is dissolved.

Serve right away.

Variation: Omit the strawberries and coconut extract for a smooth pineapple–banana shake.

Per serving:

141	Calories
4 g	Protein
1 g	Fat
31 g	Carbohydrate
37 mg	Sodium
1 mg	Cholesterol
2 g	Fiber

Piña Colada Cooler

The flavors of pineapple and coconut are just perfect for each other.

Makes 2 servings

2	tablespoons oat bran
1/3	cup nonfat dry milk
1	cup canned crushed pineapple (unsweetened), undrained
3/4	cup water
1/4	teaspoon coconut extract
2	teaspoons sugar or honey
1	cup ice cubes (10 small cubes)

In a blender container, combine oat bran and dry milk. Blend to a powder. Add remaining ingredients, *except* ice cubes. Blend until smooth.

Add ice while blending. Blend on high until ice is dissolved.

Serve right away.

Per serving:

152	Calories
6 g	Protein
1 g	Fat
33 g	Carbohydrate
63 mg	Sodium
2 mg	Cholesterol
2 g	Fiber

Peanut Butter Candy Balls

Peanut butter lovers will adore these!

Makes 12 candies

1/3	cup nonfat dry milk
1/4	cup rolled oats
3	tablespoons peanut butter, smooth or crunchy
1	teaspoon vanilla extract
1/4	teaspoon almond extract
2	tablespoons orange juice (unsweetened)
1	teaspoon sugar

In a small bowl, combine all ingredients. Mix well. Divide mixture evenly and roll into 12 balls.

Store in the refrigerator, covered.

Per candy:

41	Calories
2 g	Protein
2 g	Fat
3 g	Carbohydrate
29 mg	Sodium
0 mg	Cholesterol
1 g	Fiber

Peanut Raisin Balls

These no-bake goodies are a cross between a candy and a cookie. They're a wonderful treat to have handy for snacks.

Makes 24 candies

1/2	cup rolled oats
1/2	cup coarsely chopped peanuts (unsalted)
1/2	cup raisins
1/2	cup chopped, mixed dried fruit

Combine all ingredients in a food processor. Process until mixture is uniformly ground and starts to hold together in small clumps.

Roll into 24 one-inch balls.

Cover and chill.

Serve cold.

Per candy:

40	Calories
1 g	Protein
2 g	Fat
6 g	Carbohydrate
1 mg	Sodium
0 mg	Cholesterol
1 g	Fiber

Index

Appetizers and hors d'oeuvres
  See also Snacks; Spreads
  Oat 'n Chive Snackers, 267
  Sweet 'n Sour Meatballs, 65
Apples
  See also Fruits
  Apple Double Oat Bread, 134
  Apple Gingerbread, 196–197
  Apple Nut Bars, 212–213
  Apple Oatmeal, 19
  Apple-Prune Spice Bread, 141
  Apple Streusel Cake, 190–191
  Cranberry Apple, 237
  Kasha Apple Pudding, 232
  Steamed Apple-Oat Pudding, 227
  Steel-Cut Oats 'n Apples, 33
Applesauce
  Applesauce Cornbread, 131
  Applesauce and Oat Bran, 24
  Applesauce Oat Pancakes, 40
  Applesauce Spice Muffins, 180
Apricots
  See also Fruits
  Apricot-Raisin Oat Bars, 260
  Orange Apricot Muffins, 181

Bananas
  See also Fruits
  Banana Mini-Pancakes, 36
  Banana Oat Muffins, 179
  Banana-Pecan Oatmeal Cookies, 246
  Banana Ring, 200
  Quick Banana Betty, 234
Beans
  Bean Loaf, 88
  Bean and Oat Burgers, 85
  Black Bean Soup, 50
  Casserole, Cheddar Beans and Oats, 87
  Crockpot Oats and Beans, 121
  Easy Bean Bake, 112
  Lentil Oat Soup, 52
  "Oat-estroni" Soup, 45
  Zesty Bean Bake, 86
Blueberries
  See also Fruits
  Blueberry Muffins, 175
  Blueberry Oat Cakes, 37
Breads, 126–151
  See also Yeast Breads
  Apple Double Oat, 134
  Apple-Prune Spice, 141
  Applesauce Cornbread, 131
  Carrot Spice, 132–133
  Cheesy "Breadwiches," 146

Chili Cornbread, 145
Date Nut, 139
Fruity Oat Bran, 129
Golden Raisin, 140
Grape Nutty, 138
Ideas for, 127–128
Lemon Poppy Seed, 135
Onion 'n Oat Beer, 149
Pineapple Pecan Loaf, 130
Pumpkin Oat, 142–143
Raisin Oat Round, 144
Skillet Onion, 148
Three-Seed, 150–151
Toaster Oat, 147
Zucchini, 136–7
Breakfast Ideas, 9–42
  Almond-Oat Bran Breakfast Treat, 28
  Apple Oatmeal, 19
  Applesauce and Oat Bran, 24
  Applesauce Oat Pancakes, 40
  Banana Mini-Pancakes, 36
  Berries 'n Creme Oat Bran, 29
  Blueberry Oat Cakes, 37
  Breakfast Oatmeal Patties, 22
  Buckwheat-Oat Pancakes, 39
  Carob Oat Bran, 30
  Cornmeal Breakfast Combo, 27
  Cottage Cheese Pancakes, 38
  Creamy Wheat and Oats, 35
  Creamy Wheat Combo, 31
  Crockpot Oatmeal, 15
  Easy Duo, 32
  Granola, 16
  Granola, Hot, 17
  Italian Oatmeal Patties, 20–21
  Muesli, 12
  Oat Flour Pancakes, 42
  Orange Fruit Treat, 14
  Orange Oat Bran, 23
  Orange Oatmeal, 13A
  Overnight Cinnamon Waffles, 41
  Overnight Fruited Cereal, 34
  Peaches 'n Creme Casserole, 18
  Raisin Bran Cereal, 25
  Steel-Cut Oats 'n Apples, 33
  Yogurt and Oat Bran Breakfast, 26
Broccoli Bonanza, 104–105
Burgers
  Bean and Oat, 85
  Chili Turkey, 69
  French Turkey, 68
  Mexican Tofu, 92
  Savory Oat, 84

Cakes, 188–213
  Apple Gingerbread, 196–197
  Apple Nut Bars, 212–213
  Apple Streusel, 190–191
  Banana Ring, 200
  Carob Brownies, 202–203
  Carrot Squares, 210–211
  Cranberry Orange Cake, 208–209
  Festive Fruitcake, 198–199
  Harvest Pound, 192–193
  Honey Sweet Coffee, 206–207
  Ideas for, 189
  Pineapple Upside-Down Coffee, 204–205
  Raspberry-Almond Oat Bars, 201
  Strawberry Jam Bars, 213–214
  Sweet Potato, 194–195
Carob
  Carob Brownies, 202–203
  Carob Oat Bran, 30
Carrots
  Carrot Spice Bread, 132–133
  Carrot Squares, 210–211
  Golden Carrot Oats, 123
Casseroles
  Cheddar Beans and Oats, 87
  Company Fish, 75
  Corny, 120
  Italian Tomato, 102
  Peaches 'n Creme, 18
Cauliflower
  Cauliflower and Oats, 114
  Dusty Cauliflower, 113
Cereal
  See also Breakfast Ideas
  Apple Oatmeal, 19
  Applesauce and Oat Bran, 24
  Cornmeal Breakfast Combo, 27
  Creamy Wheat and Oats, 35
  Creamy Wheat Combo, 31
  Granola, Hot, 17
  Muesli, 12
  Orange Oatmeal, 13
  Overnight Fruited Cereal, 34
  Raisin Bran Cereal, 25
  Steel-Cut Oats 'n Apples, 33
  Yogurt and Oat Bran Breakfast, 26
Cherries
  See also Fruits
  Cherry-Berry, 235
Chicken
  See also Entrées
  Chicken Croquettes, 63
  Chicken Oat Stew, 62
  Honey Orange Chicken, 57
  Pineapple Granola Chicken, 61
  Sesame, 60
  Texas Baked, 58–59

Chili
  Chili Cornbread, 145
  Chili Oat Stew, 49
  Chili Turkey Burgers, 69
  Chili Turkey Loaf, 70
Cookies, 243–262
  Almond Granola Bars, 262
  Apricot-Raisin Oat Bars, 260
  Banana-Pecan Oatmeal, 246
  Brown Sugar Crisps, 256
  Chinese Almond, 248
  Chocolate-Almond Oat Bars, 261
  Cinnamon Oat Crisps, 252
  Cocoa Specials, 253
  Fig Bars, 254–255
  Ginger Snaps, 249
  Ideas for, 244
  Jam-Filled, 257
  Lemon Bars, 258–259
  Lemon Sesame, 250
  Molasses Fruit 'n Nut Gems, 251
  Orange Oatmeal, 245
  Peanut Oatmeal, 247
Corn
  Corn and Oat Chowder, 54
  Corn Pudding, 106
  Corn Sticks, 270
  Corny Casserole, 120
  Herbed Corn Cakes, 185
Cornbread
  Applesauce Cornbread, 131
  Chili Cornbread, 145
Cranberries
  See also Fruits
  Cranberry Apple, 237
  Cranberry Orange Cake, 208–209
Crisps, 235–242
  Cherry-Berry, 235
  Cool Orange, 238–239
  Cranberry Apple, 237
  Peach Melba Crispies, 242
  Pear Crunch, 236
  Strawberry Dessert, 240–241

Drinks
  Piña Colada Cooler, 282
  Strawberry Smoothie, 280
  Tropical Treat, 281

Entrées, 55–76
  Chicken Croquettes, 63
  Chicken Oat Stew, 62
  Chili Turkey Burgers, 69
  Chili Turkey Loaf, 70
  Company Fish Casserole, 75
  Dijon Fish Bits, 74
  Fish Cakes, 76
  French Fish Fillets, 73

French Turkey Burgers, 68
Honey Orange Chicken, 57
Ideas for, 56
Italian Cornish Hens, 64
Pineapple Granola Chicken, 61
Salmon Croquettes, 72
Sesame Chicken, 60
Sweet 'n Sour Meatballs, 65
Texas Baked Chicken, 58–59
Tuna Loaf Italiano, 71
Turkey Cutlets Italiano, 66–67

Figs
  See also Fruits
  Cinnamon Fig Muffins, 174
  Fig Bars, 254–255
Fish
  Company Fish Casserole, 75
  Dijon Fish Bits, 74
  Fish Cakes, 76
  French Fish Fillets, 73
Fruitcake, Festive, 198–199
Fruits
  See also specific kinds
  Cinnamon Fig Muffins, 174
  Date Nut Bread, 139
  Fruity Oat Bran Bread, 129
  Fruity Oat Pudding, 230
  Molasses Fruit 'n Nut Gems, 251
  Oatmeal, Fruit and Nut Bread, 156–157
  Overnight Fruited Cereal, 34
  Piña Colada Cooler, 282
  Steel-Cut Oats 'n Apples, 33
  Strawberry Jam Bars, 213–214
  Tropical Treat, 281

Italian
  Italian Cornish Hens, 64
  Italian Polenta, 82
  Italian Oatmeal Patties, 20–21
  Italian Tomato Casserole, 102
  Tuna Loaf Italiano, 71
  Turkey Cutlets Italiano, 66–67

Lemons
  See also Fruits
  Lemon Bars, 258–259
  Lemon Cheese Pie, 214–215
  Lemon Pear Muffins, 176
  Lemon Poppy Seed Bread, 135
  Lemon Sesame Cookies, 250

Meatless Entrées, 77–93
  Bean Loaf, 88
  Bean and Oat Burgers, 85
  Cheddar Beans and Oats, 87
  Ideas for, 78
  Italian Polenta, 82

Mexicali Squares, 80–81
Mexican Tofu Burgers, 92
Oat-Stuffed Peppers, 83
Oriental Sesame Tofu, 90–91
Savory Oat Burgers, 84
Spiced Cheese and Oat Loaf, 89
Tofu Oat Loaf, 93
Veggie Pan Pizza, 79
Zesty Bean Bake, 86

Mexican
  Mexicali Squares, 80–81
  Mexican Tofu Burgers, 92

Muffins, 164–187
  Applesauce Spice, 180
  Banana Oat, 179
  Blueberry, 175
  Carob Date, 184
  Cinnamon Fig, 174
  Cooked Oat Bran, 168
  Herbed Corn Cakes, 185
  Ideas for, 165
  Jelly, 182
  Lemon Pear, 176
  Oat Flour, 183
  Orange Apricot, 181
  Orange-Pecan-Currant, 169
  Original Oat Bran, 166
  Pineapple Oat Bran Cakes, 167
  Pineapple Yogurt, 171
  Pumpkin Bran, 177
  Raisin Bran, 170
  Raspberry, 173
  Spinach, 186–187
  Surprise Tomato, 178

Nuts
  Almond Granola Bars, 262
  Almond-Oat Bran Breakfast Treat, 28
  Apple Nut Bars, 212–213
  Banana-Pecan Oatmeal Cookies, 246
  Chinese Almond Cookies, 248
  Chocolate-Almond Oat Bars, 261
  Date Nut Bread, 139
  Oatmeal, Fruit and Nut Bread, 156–157
  Orange-Pecan-Currant Muffins, 169
  Peanut Oatmeal Cookies, 247
  Peanut Raisin Balls, 284
  Pineapple Pecan Loaf, 130

Oats, Forms of
  Cooking directions, 1–8
  Oat Bran, 3
  Oat Flour, 8
  Rolled Oats, 4–5
  Steel-Cut Oats, 7
  Whole Oats (Groats), 6

Oranges
   See also Fruits
   Cool Orange Crisp, 238–239
   Cranberry Orange Cake, 208–209
   Orange Apricot Muffins, 181
   Orange Fruit Treat, 14
   Orange Oat Bran, 23
   Orange Oatmeal, 13
   Orange Oatmeal Cookies, 245
   Orange-Pecan-Currant Muffins, 169
   Orange Raisin Bread, 160–161

Pancakes
   See also Breakfast Ideas
   Applesauce Oat, 40
   Banana Mini-Pancakes, 36
   Blueberry Oat Cakes, 37
   Buckwheat-Oat, 39
   Cottage Cheese, 38
   Oat Flour, 42
   Potato-Oat, 107
Peaches
   See also Fruits
   Peach Melba Crispies, 242
   Peaches 'n Creme Casserole, 18
Pears
   See also Fruits
   Lemon Pear Muffins, 176
   Pear Crunch, 236
Pie Crust
   See also Pies
   Pastry Pie Crust, 276
   Triple Crown Pie Crust, 277
Pies, 214–224
   Lemon Cheese, 214–215
   Molasses-Oatmeal Spice, 220–221
   Orange Bean, 218–219
   Party Ice Creme, 222–223
   Pineapple Cheese, 224
   Sweet Potato, 216–217
Pineapple
   See also Fruits
   Piña Colada Cooler, 282
   Pineapple Cheese Pie, 224
   Pineapple Granola Chicken, 61
   Pineapple Oat Bran Cakes, 167
   Pineapple Oat Pudding, 231
   Pineapple Pecan Loaf, 130
   Pineapple Upside-Down Coffee Cake,
      204–205
   Pineapple Yogurt Muffins, 171
Potatoes
   Cheesy Stuffed Potatoes, 108
   Potato Kugel, 109
   Potato-Oat Pancakes, 107
   Potato-Oat Soup, 46
Potpourri, 263–284
   Beer 'n Rye Rolls, 272

Corn Sticks, 272
English Tea Biscuits, 266
Garlic Oat Crackers, 268
Garlic Sticks, 269
Herbed Bread Twists, 274–275
Hummus Spread, 278
Ideas for, 264
Mushroom Pâté, 279
Oat Bran Biscuits, 273
Oat Bran Rusks, 265
Oat 'n Chive Snackers, 267
Pastry Pie Crust, 276
Peanut Butter Candy Balls, 283
Peanut Raisin Balls, 284
Piña Colada Cooler, 282
Steel-Cut Scones, 271
Strawberry Smoothie, 280
Triple Crown Pie Crust, 277
Tropical Treat, 281
Poultry
   See also Chicken; Turkey
   Italian Cornish Hens, 64
Puddings, 225–234
   Creamy Oat, 233
   Fruity Oat Pudding, 230
   Ideas for, 226
   Indian, 228
   Kasha Apple Pudding, 232
   Oat Bran Cheese, 229
   Pineapple Oat, 231
   Quick Banana Betty, 234
   Steamed Apple-Oat, 227
Pumpkin
   Pumpkin Bran Muffins, 177
   Pumpkin Oat Bread, 142–143

Raisins
   See also Fruits
   Apricot-Raisin Oat Bars, 260
   Golden Raisin Bread, 140
   Orange Raisin Bread, 160–161
   Overnight Fruited Cereal, 34
   Raisin Bran Cereal, 25
   Raisin Bran Muffins, 170
   Raisin Oat Round, 144
Raspberries
   See also Fruits
   Raspberry-Almond Oat Bars, 201
   Raspberry Muffins, 173

Salmon Croquettes, 72
Seafood
   See Fish; Salmon; Tuna
Snacks
   See also Appetizers
   Garlic Oat Crackers, 268
   Garlic Sticks, 269

Granola, 16
Oat 'n Chive Snackers, 267

Soups, 43–54
Black Bean, 50
Chili Oat Stew, 49
Corn and Oat Chowder, 54
Ideas for, 44
Lentil Oat, 52
"Oat-estroni," 45
Potato Oat, 46
Split Pea, 47

Spreads
Hummus, 278
Mushroom Pâté, 279
Sweet 'n Sour Cabbage, 51
Tomato Oatmeal, 48

Squash, Granola-Stuffed Acorn, 103

Strawberries
See also Fruits
Berries 'n Creme Oat Bran, 29
Strawberry Dessert Crisps, 240–241
Strawberry Jam Bars, 213–214
Strawberry Smoothie, 280

Sweet Potato
Cake, 194–195
Pie, 216–217
Soup, 53

Tomatoes
"Fried" Tomatoes, 101
Italian Tomato Casserole, 102
"Oat-estroni" Soup, 45
Oat-Stuffed Tomatoes, 122
Surprise Tomato Muffins, 178
Tomato Oatmeal, 48

Tuna Loaf Italiano, 71

Turkey
See also Fruits
Chili Turkey Burgers, 69
Chili Turkey Loaf, 70
French Turkey Burgers, 68
Turkey Cutlets Italiano, 66–67

Vegetables and Side Dishes, 94–125
Broccoli Bonanza, 104–105
Broiled Zucchini, 100
Cauliflower and Oats, 114
Cheesy Stuffed Potatoes, 108
Corn Pudding, 106
Corny Casserole, 120
Crockpot Oats and Beans, 121
Curried Oats, 118
Dusty Cauliflower, 113
Easy Bean Bake, 112
Eggplant Sticks, 96–97
"Fried" Tomatoes, 101
Golden Carrot Oats, 123
Granola-Stuffed Acorn Squash, 103
Herbed Oats and Wild Rice, 125
Ideas for, 95
Italian Tomato Casserole, 102
Mixed Grains, 124
Oat-Stuffed Tomatoes, 122
Onions, Mushrooms and Oats, 116
Pepper and Onion Squares, 110–111
Potato Kugel, 109
Potato-Oat Pancakes, 107
Sensational Spinach, 98–99
Sherried Orange Oats, 117
Spanish Oats, 119
Toasted Oat and Mushroom Bake, 115

Waffles, Overnight Cinnamon, 41

Yeast Breads, 152–163
See also Breads
Ideas for, 153
Multigrain, 154–155
Oatmeal, 162–163
Oatmeal, Fruit and Nut, 156–157
Orange Raisin, 160–161
Steel-Cut Sandwich Loaf, 158–159
Yogurt
Pineapple Yogurt Muffins, 171
Yogurt and Oat Bran Breakfast, 26

Zucchini
Bread, 136–7
Broiled Zucchini, 100

FILL IN AND MAIL...TODAY

PRIMA PUBLISHING & COMMUNICATIONS
P.O. Box 1260, Dept. OC
Rocklin, CA 95677

USE YOUR VISA/MC AND ORDER BY PHONE
(916) 624-5718
Mon.-Fri. 9–4 PST (12–7 EST)

Dear People,

I'd like to order copies of the following titles by Bobbie Hinman:

_____ copies of the original **Lean and Luscious**
at $13.95 each for a total of . . . . _____

_____ copies of **More Lean and Luscious**
at $13.95 each for a total of . . . . _____

_____ copies of **Oat Cuisine**
at $12.59 each for a total of . . . . _____

Subtotal	_____
Postage & Handling	$2.50
Sales Tax	_____
TOTAL (U.S. funds only)	_____

☐ Check enclosed for $_____, payable to Prima Publishing
Charge my ☐ Mastercard ☐ Visa

Account No. _____ Exp. Date _____

Signature _____

Your Name _____

Address _____

City/State/Zip _____

Daytime Telephone _____

GUARANTEE
YOU MUST BE SATISFIED!
You get a 30-day, 100% money-back guarantee on all books.

Thank you for your order.